NATURAL WONDERS
·OF·THE·WORLD·

DR ADRIAN GLOVER

ARCTURUS

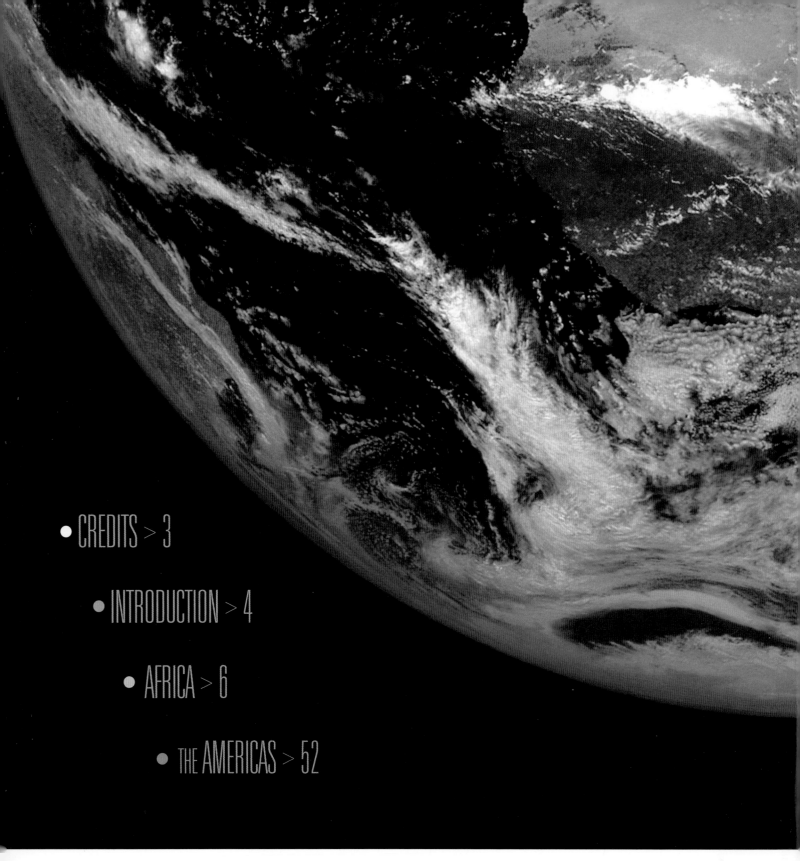

Arcturus Publishing Limited
26/27 Bickels Yard
151–153 Bermondsey Street
London SE1 3HA

Published in association with
foulsham

W. Foulsham & Co. Ltd,
The Publishing House, Bennetts Close,
Cippenham,
Slough, Berkshire SL1 5AP, England

ISBN 0-572-03165-3
This edition printed in 2005
Copyright © 2005 Arcturus Publishing Limited

British Library Cataloguing-in-Publication Data:
a catalogue record for this book is available
from the British Library

Printed in China

Jacket and book design: Steve Flight
Project editor: Belinda Jones
Layout: Talking Design

With thanks to the following picture libraries for permission to reproduce the following images:

Arcticphoto: 227

Corbis: 4, 6-7, 9, 15, 17, 20, 21, 25, 29, 31, 33, 34, 37, 41, 45, 47, 80, 81, 83, 91, 95, 104, 105, 107, 111, 115, 119, 126-127, 129, 131, 135, 139, 141, 143, 144, 145, 147, 155, 165, 177, 179, 183, 195, 197, 199, 215, 216, 217, 219, 121, 222, 225, 231, 232-233, 235, 245, 251, 253

FLPA: 5, 23, 27, 48, 49, 52-53, 55, 57, 59, 63, 65, 70, 72, 73, 75, 77, 79, 82, 85, 89, 117, 123, 125, 133, 148, 149, 151,153, 159, 163, 169, 175, 193, 201, 203, 207, 221, 229, 237, 243, 255

Getty: 43 (*National Geographic*), 120 (*Time and Life*), 173 (*AFP*)

Nature Picture Library: 35, 103, 187, 189, 223

NHPA: 13, 19, 39, 51, 61, 67, 71, 93, 97, 99, 101, 109, 113, 157, 161, 167, 171, 181, 185, 190-191, 205, 209, 211, 213, 256 (detail)

Oxford Science Library: 11, 87, 137

Science Photo Library: 69, 239, 241, 247, 249

I would like to thank Victoria Herridge for her help with both the research and writing of the text.

This book is dedicated to the memory of Andy Lamarque.

INTRODUCTION

Natural wonders are the creation of nature and its timeless processes, but it is in our minds that they become wondrous: the natural phenomena that have been selected and feature in this book are those that inspire true amazement in the human imagination. Knowing that a waterfall is the highest in the world is an interesting fact, but it is our perception of the elemental beauty of a 800-metre high (2600 feet) waterfall, deep in a remote and primeval jungle, that creates true feelings of awe.

Some travellers may be disappointed when they first observe one of the natural wonders they have read about. Expectations can destroy imagination and appreciation. Guidebooks exaggerate, and tourist

brochures even more so. Added to this, each observer will also have his or her own idea of what constitutes a natural wonder: most people would agree that the Grand Canyon is a wonder of the natural world, but is it any more so than the quiet tranquillity of a bluebell wood in springtime?

To rank the natural wonders included in this book would be impossible. We could try to rate them, but each criterion would bring its own problems. Therefore, the wonders in this book are grouped into six geographical locations, with two themes running through each of the groups: geology and evolution.

Each wonder has been formed by these two great physical processes of the planet: geology, the gravitational energy that drives the earth's plates and creates volcanism; and evolution, the continual change, emergence and disappearance of the great lineages of life.

Each wonder is a window into the power of these great processes.

There is also great variety in the scale of both the geological and evolutionary wonders. Geology has

created the single waterfall — perhaps the result of water flowing for millions of years over a single, tiny imperfection in the rock strata — but also the immense Antarctic ice sheet.

The process of evolution has, over millenia, created the great ecosystems of the world. In the tropics the action of a tiny, almost microscopic animal known as coral has created one of the planet's wonders of biodiversity, a coral reef, whilst on land, the growth of rainforest in the warm, humid regions of Central Africa and South America has allowed speciation (the mechanism of evolution) to flourish.

Another point worth considering is who the discoverers of the natural wonders of the world were. The European explorers who set off to find the source of the Nile? Amundsen and Scott, the polar explorers?

The colonial surveyors who measured the height of great mountains? Many of these wonders were 'discovered' in places where local, indigenous people were already well aware of their significance: Ayers Rock, now known by the name of Uluru, has inspired wonder and legend in the indigenous tribes of central Australia for perhaps more than 50,000 years; long before western explorers had reached the country's shores.

This book is a tour of the numerous types of natural wonders to be found on earth, but the ultimate tour can only be achieved by visiting these places and seeing, feeling and understanding their inimitability for yourself — experiencing them today, and reflecting on the immense past that created these wonders of the natural world.

AFRICA

The word Africa conjures up images of discovery and exploration, of unnavigated rivers disappearing into dark, forbidding jungles, of vast, rolling savannahs and of even vaster deserts. More than any other continent, Africa epitomizes the spirit of adventure. At 30,365,000 square kilometres (11,724, 000 square miles), it is the second largest continent in the world after Asia, and the only continent that is bisected by both the equator and the 0° meridian line. It is a continent of great cultural, biological and geological diversity, so it is unsurprising that so many of the world's natural wonders are found there. Africa can be said to have changed the world: it is the cradle of humanity, the place where the human species originated before dispersing across the globe, and the fossils of our ancestors are predominantly found there.

Africa's geology is dominated by the Great Rift Valley fault system that threatens to split the land in two. This system produces the mighty peaks of the east as well as volcanoes throughout the continent. In addition to possessing the unpredictable and ever changing landscape of a tectonically active region, Africa has also seen major changes in its climate over the last few million years. It has become drier and hotter, and the desert belts have grown enormously.

The incredible geology of Africa is undisputed, and the great rivers, lakes, mountains and waterfalls are wonders in their own right. However, many of Africa's natural wonders are evolutionary in origin, with the continent's geological features providing a spectacular backdrop to some of the world's most unique and fragile ecosystems. Consequently, Africa's geological wonders can rarely be discussed without also referring to the creatures that live there. This interplay between biology and geology could be said to be the true wonder of Africa. The stately solidity of rock formations and the power of volcanism and water are wonders in themselves, but are immeasurably enhanced by the dynamic and more transient beauty of the teeming life forms of this mesmerizing continent.

THE SINGING SANDS

Filling nearly all of North Africa, the Sahara is the largest desert in the world. It covers 8,600,000 square kilometres (3,320,500 square miles), stretching from the Atlantic Ocean to the Red Sea. The Atlas Mountains mark its northern borders and to the south it ends in ancient, unmoving sand dunes. Only 25 per cent of the Sahara is actually covered by sand sheets or dunes; the rest is made up of rocky plateaux and gravel-covered plains, containing volcanoes, lakes, rivers and oases. However, it would be unwise to assume that this variety of environments makes the Sahara a hospitable place. Despite evidence that humans have been scratching out an existence along its infrequent waterways and oases for thousands of years, the arid interior remains something of a mystery. The desert, with its 300-metre (985 feet) high dunes that are heard to 'sing' and boom out as the wind blows over them, still represents an almost impenetrable barrier to humanity.

The sands of the Erg Chigaga desert, Morocco, lie within the Sahara Desert, the largest in the world. Although dry, the desert is only one-quarter sand dunes

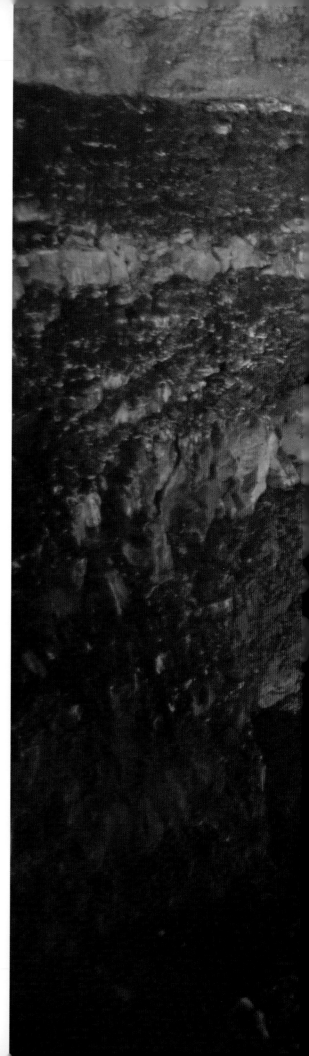

DEEP HEAT

At the northern end of Africa's Great Rift Valley you can stand 116 metres (380 feet) below sea level, yet not get your feet wet. The Danakil Depression in Ethiopia is the hottest place on earth; temperatures of 63°C (145°F) have been recorded. The remnant of an evaporated inland sea, this low-lying plain stretches 1,200 square kilometres (460 square miles). This arid land is cut off from the Red Sea by a chain of active volcanoes; no water flows in or out and any that falls simply evaporates. Ethiopia's most active volcano, Erta Ale, is found there, and the Danakil Depression also contains Africa's lowest volcanoes – open vents of bubbling lava many metres below sea level. Lava lakes, earthquakes and the elemental plains of raw sulphur create this bleak, yet stunning, example of the earth's raw beauty.

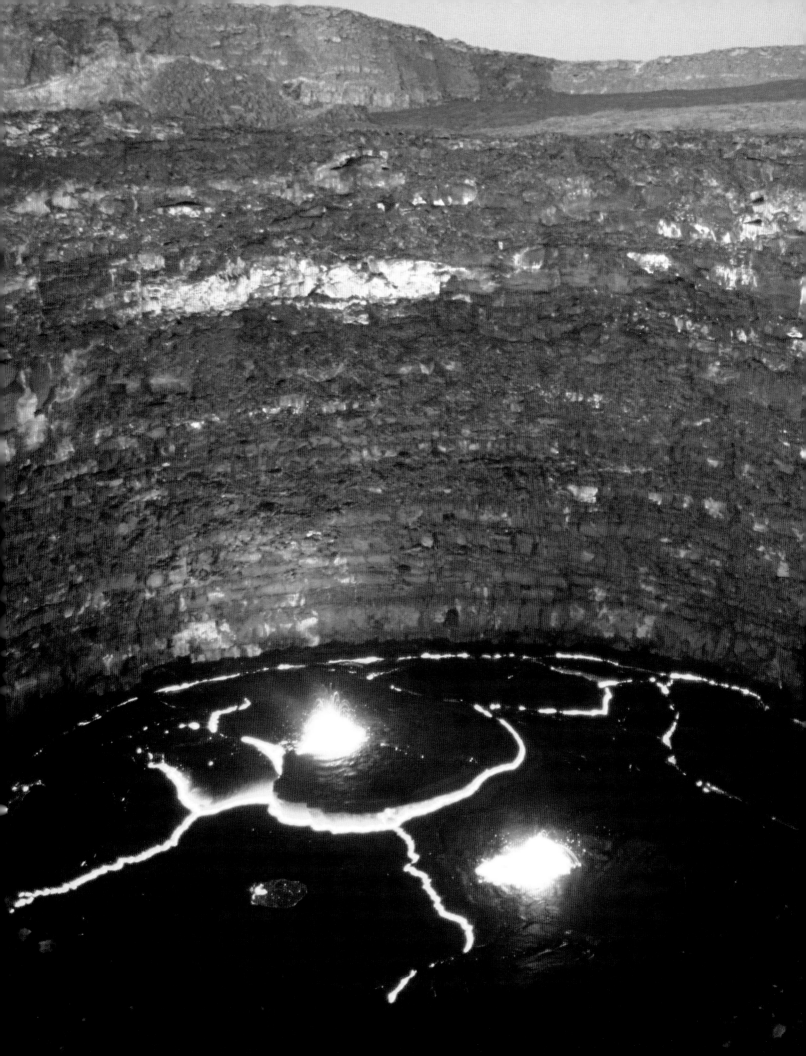

LAND OF LAVA, FOREST AND ICE

Virunga National Park is undoubtedly one of the most diverse regions of the terrestrial world, containing within its borders lakes, marshes, savannahs, lava flows, tropical rainforest and glaciated peaks. It straddles the border of the Democratic Republic of Congo and Rwanda, and is contiguous with the Rwenzori Mountains of Uganda, where permanent glaciers and cloud hide 5,119-metre (16, 800 feet) high Mount Stanley. Huge populations of hippopotamus, elephant and antelope are found in the lower regions, and in the higher reaches the elusive mountain gorilla can be found in the cloud forests of dormant volcanoes such as Mount Sabinyo. In the west, the dangerous Nyriragongo volcano is still active, producing the fastest flowing lava in the world; it erupted in 2002, destroying parts of the town of Goma.

The heavily forested slopes of Mount Sabinyo lie within the Virunga National Park, straddling the borders of Rwanda and the Democratic Republic of Congo. The region is thickly covered by rainforest, and is home to the rare mountain gorilla

SMOKE THAT THUNDERS

The mighty waterfalls of the world compete for superlatives – the largest water volume, the highest, the most beautiful – but none can compare with the shocking chasm that the Zambezi River has cut through ancient basalt rocks. The Victoria Falls discharge some 950 cubic metres (260,000 gallons) of water per second over the lip of the gorge; their winning statistic: the 1,700-metre (5,600 feet) width of the falls themselves. Over millions of years, linear fault lines in the basalt have been explored and eroded by water to create a spectacle witnessed by Africans for millennia, and western explorers since the nineteenth century. The Kalolo-Lozi people named it *Mosi-oa-Tunya*, meaning 'smoke that thunders', for the characteristic veil of mist that hangs above it, visible for many miles around. The falls' influence extends beyond the gorge itself; they support a unique rainforest environment of acacia, teak and ivory palm, providing an oasis amid the otherwise arid savannah.

Victoria Falls, on the border of Zimbabwe and Zambia. The great force of water creates a veil of mist that hangs in the air, and feeds a miniature rainforest environment along the lip of the gorge

THE CELESTIAL MOUNTAIN

Table Mountain, at 3,000 metres (9,850 feet) wide and 1,086 metres (3,550 feet) tall, dominates the Cape Peninsula at its northern end. Its distinctive flat-topped profile, the result of almost perfectly horizontal layers of sandstone exposed by weathering, overlooks Cape Town in South Africa. The face of Table Mountain is a stark wall scarred with crevasses, in dramatic contrast with the incredibly diverse fynbos flora on the summit plateau. The plateau is criss-crossed by streams and valleys; the cloud cover, or 'tablecloth', that forms rapidly over the mountain when the wind blows from the southeast maintains this lush region. Rock hyrax, baboons, snakes and tortoises all live on the mountainside. Table Mountain was first officially climbed in 1503, and since then it has epitomized the Cape region and inspired artistic and scientific endeavour. It is the only geological feature on earth to have a constellation named after it – Mensa (which means 'table' in Latin), named by Nicolas de Lacaille in the eighteenth century. The constellation is visible in the southern hemisphere in July.

The lesser flamingo,
Phoenicopterus minor,
feeding in the shallow waters
of Lake Natron, Tanzania.
The water is caustic to the
touch, yet the flamingos
can feed on the abundant
bacteria that are found there

PINK SODA

Lake Natron is like no other place on earth. Its warm waters, fed by hot springs, are full of sodium carbonate and are caustic to the touch; alkaline salt crusts form upon its surface. No rivers flow in or out of Lake Natron and, consequently, the water level changes seasonally, exposing mud flats that can become as hot as 50°C (122°F). Despite its waters being as alkaline as ammonia with a pH of 10.5, life can still be found in Lake Natron. The lesser flamingo can withstand the caustic waters, and uses this ability to avoid predation from the less tolerant carnivores. Lake Natron is the only regular breeding ground of the lesser flamingo in the world, and these birds feed on the billions of salt-loving spirulina bacteria that thrive there. The bacteria contain pigments that dye the flamingos and the salty crust of the lake pink and red, creating a remarkable colour spectacle that can be seen from space.

Palm trees grow in the floodplains of the Nile River in Egypt. The river feeds Africa's most fertile soils, allowing agriculture to flourish

RIVER OF DARKNESS

Stretching for 6,650 kilometres (4,150 miles), the Nile is the longest river in the world. Rising in Uganda and flowing out from Lake Victoria, it meanders its way northwards through nine African countries before emptying into the Mediterranean Sea. The ancient Egyptians called it *Ar*, meaning black, and signifying darkness, and the search for the Nile's source led many explorers along its banks of black mud into the dark reaches of the African jungle. The Nile Basin comprises a tenth of the area of Africa and has supported human life for millennia. The river is inextricably linked with ancient Egyptian civilization and mythology, but it is equally important in Africa today. The Nile Delta contains Africa's most fertile soil, made up of silt washed down from Ethiopia. With the river's year-round offering of abundant water, together with the warmth of the local climate, agriculture flourishes along the Nile's entire length.

The Nile not only supports human life in these arid lands — it is also a crucial means of transport, meaning that people can live more easily beside it

GREAT RIFT VALLEY

Arguably one of the most impressive single geographic features on the planet, the Great Rift Valley has provided Africa with the greatest volcanoes and the deepest lakes on the continent. Over 5,000 kilometres (3,100 miles) in length and stretching from the River Jordan and the Dead Sea to central Mozambique, the valley is an active example of plate tectonics. The formation of the valley still continues, and in a few million years – almost nothing in geological terms – the whole of eastern Africa will be split off from the rest of the continent and a new ocean created. In Africa, the rift is split into eastern and western courses, with the western rift, which borders Uganda, Congo and Tanzania, giving birth to the continent's greatest mountain ranges – the Rwenzoris, Mitumbas and Virungas. It is also here that the continent's deepest lake is found. At 1,470 metres (4,800 feet) deep, Lake Tanganyika is second only in depth – of the world's freshwater lakes – to Lake Baikal in Siberia. Paradoxically, this geologically violent region is an area of outstanding biology; it is home not just to the giant herbivores and predators of the savannah, but is also a treasure trove of remains of human beings' ancient ancestors – the birthplace of humanity itself.

The Rift Valley, at Lake Manyara, Tanzania. The Rift Valley is one of the greatest geological features on the planet, with the whole of Eastern Africa gradually splitting from the rest of the continent — in only a few million years, a new ocean may be formed here

THE JADE SEA

The world's largest permanent desert lake, with a surface area of 6,405 square kilometres (2,470 square miles), is Lake Turkana. Situated in Kenya with its northern tip just within Ethiopia, the lake's rich green waters are fed by three rivers, the Omo, Turkwel and Kerio. Known locally as the Jade Sea, Lake Turkana is the most saline of Africa's large lakes. It has no river outlets, but thousands of years ago it was joined with Lake Baringo to form a much larger body of water, flowing onwards to the Nile. This ancient water connection has left its mark; Nile perch still remain, as does the Nile crocodile – over 12,000 live on the volcanic central island. In the rolling volcanic hills that flank the lake, on the slopes of Mount Sibiloi, is a 7 million-year-old petrified forest. Lake Turkana is surrounded by echoes of the distant past; its shores were once home to our human ancestors, and fossils continue to be discovered there.

DUNES OF THE VAST
DESERT

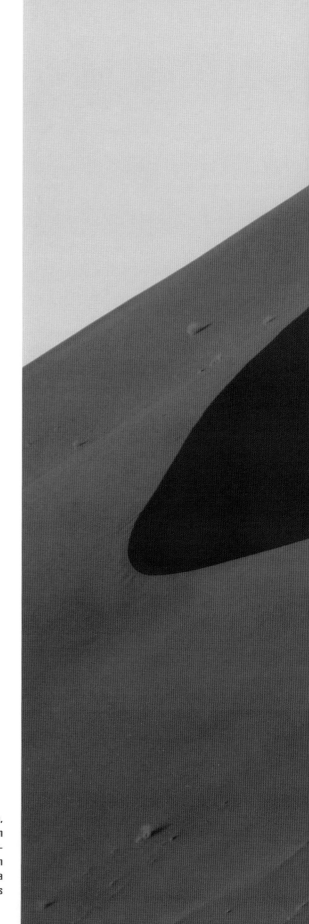

Namib means vast in the Nama language, and this great expanse of orange sand, sculpted into seemingly endless, phantasmagorical dunes, certainly lives up to its name. Stretching from Angola in the north down to South Africa, this 50,000 square kilometres (19,300 square miles) of parched land makes up one of the world's oldest and richest deserts. The desert runs along the Atlantic coastline for 1,600 kilometres (990 miles), and the dense fog that rolls in off the ocean provides moisture that sustains an ancient and diverse ecosystem among the inhospitable dunes. The dunes of the Namib are the oldest in the world, and also the largest. These incredible and ever growing structures can reach 340 metres (1,115 feet) in height, and are blown into razor-sharp ridges that stretch for miles. Shipwrecks, victims of Namibia's treacherous Skeleton Coast, have been found in the desert some 50 metres (165 feet) inland, a testament to the slow but relentless encroachment of the desert upon the Atlantic Ocean.

At Sossusvlei, Namibia, a sand dune glows in the morning light. The ever-shifting structures are blown by the wind into a vast sea of ridges

LAKE OF SHINING WATERS

Lake Nyasa, the most southerly of all the lakes in the Great Rift Valley, contains more species of fish in its gloriously clear waters than any other lake in the world. Over 500 fish species are found within its 29,600 square kilometres (11,400 miles) of tropical waters, 400 of which are cichlid fish endemic to the lake. The enigmatic *mbuna* (rock fish) are found there, whose total species numbers and evolutionary relationships are unknown to science. Although Lake Nyasa appears to be a stretch of uniformly beautiful blue water, crystal clear and sparkling, it actually contains a vast range of different watery habitats – from sand to rock to reed beds. Its waters are permanently layered into regions of different temperatures, from the cool bottom layers to the warm surface. Such underwater variability, and the lake's 1-2 million year history, are thought to be responsible for the massive amount of evolution and speciation – the formation of entirely new biological species – that has occurred there.

Sunrise over Lake Nyasa, the most southerly of the Rift Valley lakes. The clear blue waters of the lake hide a great complexity of life that scientists have only recently begun to understand

Rock formations on the shores of Lake Victoria, Tanzania. The largest of the African lakes, and the second largest freshwater lake in the world, Lake Victoria is home to over 800 species of fish

THE GREAT LAKE

Lake Victoria, the greatest of the African lakes, straddles the border of Uganda, Kenya and Tanzania; its 68,000-kilometre square (26,250 square miles) surface makes it the second largest freshwater lake in the world. It was first sighted by European explorers in 1858, when John Hanning Speke journeyed north from Lake Tanganyika in a bid to find the source of the River Nile. The leader of the expedition, Richard Francis Burton, was left ill in Tanzania, and Speke later claimed the discovery for himself, fuelling a bitter row. Over evolutionary time, isolation has created a unique ecosystem; over 800 species of cichlid fish have been discovered in the region. Rich volcanic soils, plentiful rainfall and the abundant aquatic life have created one of the most populated regions of Africa, with 107 million people living in the area.

FLOWERS OF THE CAPE

The world is divided into six great floral kingdoms, and at the southern tip of Africa lies its richest, the fynbos, or Cape floral kingdom. *Fynbos* is the Afrikaans word for fine bush and, on the thin, well-drained soils of the southern African uplands, an incredible 8,700 species of shrub-size plants have been recorded. Of these, over 6,000 are known to be endemic to the region. A visitor to the fynbos might easily discover over a hundred species just a stone's throw from a single spot; low productivity in the soil, coupled with regular fires, mean that fast-growing species do not have time to out-compete the slower growing ones, maintaining biodiversity over ecological time. To the agriculturalist, thin, infertile soils are undesirable, but for an ecologist, they help to maintain the extraordinary diversity of the fynbos.

Flowers of the fynbos biome in South Africa. Fynbos is the most species-rich biome in the world, and is found in the thin, well-drained soils of the southern African uplands

A baby mountain gorilla feeding in the forests of Uganda. The mountain gorilla, *Gorilla gorilla berengei*, is endangered by local population pressure on its natural habitat

IMPENETRABLE FOREST

With valleys engulfed by vines, and shrubs growing so densely that travel is slow and laborious, Bwindi Impenetrable National Park is aptly named. Bwindi is incredibly rich in plants and wildlife. The park has over 200 species of tree, 100 species of fern, 336 bird species, 202 species of butterfly and 120 species of mammal. These impressive statistics add up to the richest fauna and flora in East Africa. This exceptionally high biodiversity may be because Bwindi spans the boundary between lowland and montane vegetation, unusual in East African forests. Bwindi is home to over 300 mountain gorillas – a third of the worldwide population of these elusive and highly endangered creatures. Its impenetrable nature means that the region remains mysterious, with the promise of many new species awaiting discovery. With little access and steep mountainsides that make logging difficult, it may be hoped that Bwindi will continue to thrive, protecting the vast number of unique and endangered species that live there.

Bwindi Impenetrable Park lies in the mountainous central regions of Africa, close to the borders of Rwanda and the Democratic Republic of Congo. The thick, species-rich forest is home to many rare species

ENDLESS PLAINS

The Serengeti Plain is the last remaining example of a Pleistocene large mammal ecosystem. The plains of rolling hills, grasslands, woodlands and granitic outcrops, called kopjes, are home to 1.6 million herbivorous ungulates – mainly wildebeests, gazelles, zebras, buffalo – and their predators. The Serengeti is the only place in Africa where annual herbivore migrations still take place, and is by far the largest of the great national parks. Its richness is a result of the layers of volcanic ash laid down by Great Rift Valley volcanoes over the millennia. The Maasai people have grazed their cattle in this paradise for thousands of years and call it Siringitu, the place where the land moves on forever. This 30,000-kilometre square (11,590 square miles) ecosystem is also one of the oldest on earth and, at Olduvai Gorge in the eastern Serengeti, human and pre-human hominid remains go back 2 million years.

The Serengeti Plains afford views of the sky and land that roll away uninterrupted into the distance, only to merge at the horizon an unimaginable distance away. A fitting birthplace for the species that colonized most of the planet's lands; *Homo erectus*

Mount Kilimanjaro rises
above the plains of
East Africa in Amboseli
National Park, Kenya.
This high peak is the
largest volcano in the
world, and is thought
to still be active

SHINING MOUNTAIN

The wonder of Mount Kilimanjaro lies in its improbability. East Africa appears uniquely blessed by awesome giants of nature – the great herbivores of the Serengeti Plain, Lake Victoria, the Great Rift Valley. It seems almost excessive that the area should also be home to this 6-kilometre (19,685 feet) high giant of the volcanoes, the tallest in the world. Kilimanjaro is still erupting – fumaroles line its highest peak, Kibo. Scientists have warned of future eruptions – molten lava is thought to lie only a few hundred metres below its summit. Climbers routinely scale this peak, following the easy line of the summit cone, yet its great height poses the danger of altitude sickness to the unwary. The 40,000 who attempt it each year are rewarded with a journey through unique and bizarre climatic zones. Giant lobelias, *Lobelia deckenii*, line the paths that move through cloud forest and woods of giant heather, before finally ending at the icy, glaciated cone of smoking Kibo.

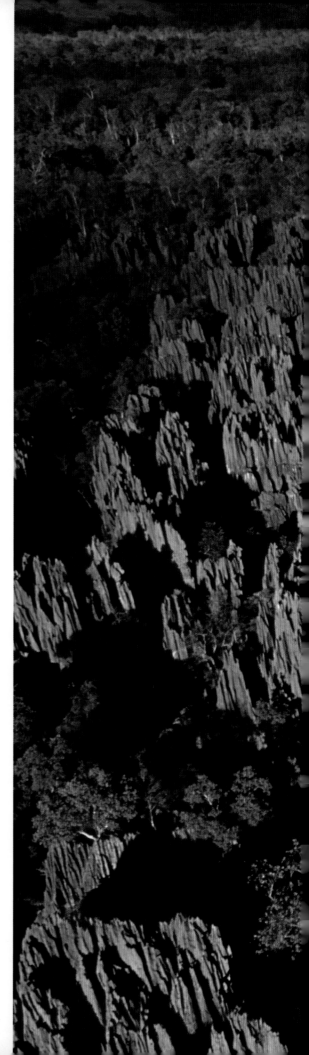

THE PETRIFIED FOREST

The deciduous forests of Tsingy de Bemaraha in Madagascar are home to a variety of strange and rare beasts. Many of Madagascar's enigmatic lemur species are found here, and the highly unusual and elusive aye-aye. This nocturnal creature is considered a diabolical beast by the Malagasy and, with its huge, staring eyes and long, bony middle fingers and toes, it seems fitting that it should be found in the equally fantastical Tsingy region. The Bemaraha Plateau occupies most of the area, and the rough, limestone terrain of this massif — a central mountain mass — is so dissected by erosion that accessibility is near impossible. Extensive pinnacle formations soar above the vegetation, like tightly packed needles, creating a forest of rocks that has proved impenetrable to exploration. Only the great Manambolo Gorge, with its vertical walls 400 metres (1,310 feet) deep, appears to have encouraged human endeavour, and ancient burial sites abound there. The rest of the area remains an enigma to science, holding untold secrets within its rocky interior.

THE MOUNTAIN OF GOD

Ol Doinyo Lengai is Swahili for 'mountain of God'. This simmering volcanic cone stands sentinel over Lake Natron, the largest flamingo breeding colony in Africa. It is the last in a line of calderas that begins with Ngorongoro Crater to the south, and is the most active of all the Great Rift Valley volcanoes. It is the only volcano in the world to produce the low-temperature lava known as natrocarbonatite lava. At only 510°C (950°F), less than half that of more common basaltic lavas, it is not even hot enough to glow red in the daytime. Instead, Ol Doinyo Lengai produces black lava that can flow like water and cools to a sparkling, crystal-filled solid. Reactions with water vapour in the air turn this black rock white, then finally into the soft, brown powder that coats the mountain's slopes. At 2,878 metres (9,445 feet), Ol Doinyo Lengai may be overshadowed in height by nearby Kilimanjaro, but its spectacular lava, which can spray and flow like whitewater, and continual eruptions make it worthy of its name.

In the summit of Ol Doinyo Lengai, lava fountains harden in mid-air, then shatter like glass. This low-temperature 'natrocarbonatite' lava is only found on this volcano

THE GREATEST SAFARI

Safari is the Swahili word for journey, and the journey of the giant herbivores of the Serengeti and Maasai Mara is one of the greatest. It is not a single migration, but an almost continuous movement of large ungulates, mainly wildebeest and zebra. The reasons for the migration lie in the alternating wet and dry seasons of Central Africa. Migration has major ecological consequences – large, mobile animals can exploit a greater range of resources than would be possible if they were small or less mobile. From December to March, the wildebeest are concentrated in the lush, rain-ripened grasslands of the Serengeti, but as these resources are used up, they start to migrate north and west towards the Maasai Mara. From July to August, they remain in the Maasai, but by November the grasslands in the north start to dry and the animals return south to the Serengeti.

Wildebeest migrate across the Serengeti Plains in Tanzania. Wildebeest are the great herbivores of the Serengeti, and migrate from here across many obstacles to the Maasai Mara during the change from wet to dry seasons

SIMIEN NATIONAL PARK

In the western Simien mountains, bisected by the mighty Mayshasha River, Simien National Park is one of Ethiopia's hidden wonders and most fragile ecosystems. The region is home to unique species such as the Simien wolf and the walia ibex, as well as spotted hyena, bushbuck, colobus monkey and the most terrestrial of all primates, the gelada baboon. The incredible biodiversity and a range of habitats, from high montane forest to savannah and moorland, are all found among spectacular scenery. Erosion of the igneous basalt mountains over the last 25 million years has produced precipitous cliffs and gorges, with sheer walls dropping 1,500 metres (4,920 feet) into the valleys below. The jagged mountain range within Simien's territory boasts Ethiopia's highest mountain, Ras Dashan Terara. The park ranges in altitude from 1,900 metres (6,235 feet) to the 4,620-metre (15,155 feet) high tip of this lofty peak, and it is this wide variation in altitude combined with the extreme topography of the cliffs and gorges that have created and maintained this region's biodiversity.

CRATER OF LIFE

Among the undulating highlands that sweep up from the east of the Serengeti is the Ngorongoro Crater. Inactive, it is one of the world's largest and most perfect calderas – a large, basin-shaped crater formed by the collapse or explosion of the cone. This grassy realm, 19 kilometres (12 miles) in diameter and rimmed by the 600-metre (1,965 feet) high crater walls, hosts large populations of wildebeest, zebra, eland and gazelle – ample prey for the lions that also live there. The crater walls also offer refuge to a tiny population of black rhino, numbering perhaps 14 individuals – a tiny relic of this once widespread and majestic species. From the rim, where buffalo and elephants walk and leopards prowl, one can look down upon unspoilt natural beauty. No humans have made their home here; it is a place that can truly be called an animal kingdom.

Ngorongoro Crater, in the north of Tanzania, is one of the world's largest calderas. Within the walls of the crater, large populations of wildebeest and zebra roam, prey to one of the densest lion populations in the world

MOUNTAIN OF WHITENESS

An extinct 3 million-year-old stratovolcano – a steep, conical volcano built by the eruption of viscous lava flows – Mount Kenya straddles the equator in East Africa and is the second highest mountain on the continent. The local Kikuyu revere it as the home of the omnipotent deity Ngai, and name it *Kirinyaga*, meaning 'mountain of whiteness'. The twin summits of Nelion and Batian, at 5,188 and 5,199 metres (17,020 and 17,055 feet) respectively, are attainable by direct technical rock climbs via 12 small glaciers and numerous rock faces. The slightly lower Point Lenana, at 4,985 metres (16,355 feet), is reachable by trekkers whose ascent takes them through a variety of ecological habitats. From its base, savannah grassland gives way to dense forests of cedar, yellow-wood and bamboo up to 3,000 metres (16,355 feet). Above that, mosses and lichens dominate the Afro-alpine vegetation before giving way to rock and ice at bleak summits. In 1997 the mountain was awarded UNESCO World Heritage status.

THE AMERICAS

The Americas are made up of two continents, North America and South America. Together they stretch from within the Arctic Circle in the north to just outside the Antarctic Circle in the south. Despite being one continuous landmass, the clearly apparent differences between the natural wonders of these regions reflect both the enormous latitudinal span of the two continents and their distinct geological and biological evolutions.

Until around 4–5 million years ago a large channel separated these continents, allowing water to pass between the Pacific and Atlantic Oceans via the Central American Seaway. At this time the closure of the Isthmus of Panama joined North and South America, and produced something of the topology we are familiar with today. Worldwide ramifications followed: the salinity of the two oceans, which before had been roughly equal, began to diverge, with the Atlantic becoming saltier. The Gulf Stream current flowing northeast from the Gulf of Mexico in the Atlantic grew in strength, and a global circulation current called the Ocean Conveyor began to affect the earth's climate. This event has been linked to the formation of the Arctic ice sheet, which only formed some 2–3 million years ago, compared with a 30 million year origin for Antarctic ice.

North America has the oldest rocks in the world in its lowland interior shield region, dating back 4 billion years, and is unusual in that this central continental area is encircled by younger rocks and mountains on both the east and west. South America has older shield rock on its larger, eastern side, comprising the plateaux and basins of the rainforest regions. The west coast is dominated by the Andean backbone of much younger mountains.

Both North and South America are areas of high tectonic activity and extreme volcanism. The great age of these continents has meant that a vast number of incredible geological features has been sculpted over millennia. The impact of humans in both regions is notable, but there are still vast swathes of wilderness left to explore. There is no doubt that the Americas hold some of the world's most exciting natural treasures.

MONUMENT TO TIME

Cut deep by the Colorado River, the Grand Canyon is more than just a gorge – it is the most spectacular canyon in the world, winding for 445 kilometres (225 miles) across the Arizona landscape and over 1.5 kilometres (1 mile) deep in places. From the rim you can look down on the tips of mountains that are themselves ensconced within the gorge. It is a window into the distant past, exposing rocks that are up to 2 billion years old, evidence of the seas, swamps and deserts that existed here over the eons. It took 6 million years of erosion and geological activity to create this place of breathtaking drops, tumbling white water rapids and awesome waterfalls. The continual flow of the Colorado means that the canyon is still a work-in-progress and, as the years pass, will continue to get ever deeper and, no doubt, ever more majestic.

Looking down into the Grand Canyon, Arizona, from the south rim of the canyon. The Grand Canyon has been gouged out of the Arizona desert by the Colorado River, exposing rocks up to 2 billion years old

ATLANTIC JUNGLE

In south-east Brazil the great crystalline rock escarpment, the Serra do Mar, runs for 1,500 kilometres (930 miles) along the Atlantic coast, and is home to one of the country's most spectacular rainforest regions, the Mata Atlântica. These mountains form the boundary between Brazil's vast interior and the coastal cities, and it was not until the nineteenth century that the new railways took people and development across it. When Brazil was discovered by Europeans in the sixteenth century, this great escarpment was covered by dense rainforest; today there are only remnants such as the Serra dos Orgaos National Park, which gets its name, meaning 'Organ Hills', from the resemblance of the mountain pinnacles to the organs of church cathedrals. The most famous mountain in the park is the *Dedo de Deus*, meaning 'Finger of God', which rises to 1,692 metres (5,550 feet) in height and appears on the coat of arms for the state of Rio de Janeiro.

The granite mountains of the Serra do Mar act as a natural barrier between Brazil's interior and its coast; the unique 'Atlantic forests' now remain only in some areas

Sunlight filters into a narrow slot canyon, in Antelope Canyon, Arizona. The red Navajo sandstone has been eroded by flash floods for centuries, producing spectacular rock formations hidden within the desert sands

CANYON OF SHADOWS

Amid the desert sands of Arizona, sculpted from the red Navajo sandstone, the slot canyons of Antelope Creek are where nature's destructive beauty could be said to reach its zenith. The walls of Upper and Lower Antelope Canyon are, at 40 metres (130 feet) deep, just shallow enough to allow sunlight to penetrate. It is the delicate interplay between the shifting rays of the sun as it passes overhead and the sensuous curves and spirals of the sandstone formations within that transform these narrow ravines into a place of ethereal beauty. The shadows and relief of the sharp ridges contrast with the ephemeral glow of the rock, illuminated as it is in shades of red, orange and gold. The swirling sandstone formations are the result of the flash floods that tear through the area year after year, gouging out the soft sedimentary rock. While these floods leave behind new and spectacular formations, they also destroy indiscriminately, claiming the lives of many of the unwary who have come to admire their awesome beauty.

TOWERS OF PATAGONIA

The giant monoliths of the Torres del Paine dominate the northern region of Patagonia. Formed of granite and capped in a darker layer of sandstone, their unique geological structure and the forces of glacial erosion have created a climber's playground, and a unique biosphere that attracts tourists the world over. The Central Tower of Paine, at 3,400 metres (11,155 feet), represents a unique climbing challenge, and was first conquered by the British climbing pair of Don Whillans and Chris Bonnington in 1963 – with an Italian team just hours behind them. The towers, and the Grey, Tyndall and Balmaceda glaciers that tumble from them, have created a unique region of glacial grey lakes, icebergs, crags and peaks that inspire both trekkers and climbers alike. The unique fauna of the region includes the elusive rhea and the more common guanaco, closely related to the llama.

An *Anarthrophyllum desideratum* shrub flowers amidst the dramatic scenery of Torres del Paine National Park, Chile. The monoliths in the background are formed from granite, but are capped by a sandstone layer. This unique geology has been shaped by glaciers to create a renowned 'climber's playground'

FALLING ANGEL

The bizarre flat-topped mountains, or tepuís, of the Guiana Highlands rise vertically out of the rainforest of south-eastern Venezuela. It is here that the Churún River free-falls over the edge of Auyán tepuí to form the tallest free-flowing waterfall in the world – Angel Falls. Fifteen times the height of Niagara Falls, the near-vertical sides of the tepuí mean that the water can drop the entire height of the mountain.

Despite their size, the Angel Falls were not widely known to the world until the mid-twentieth century. A gold prospector, James Angel, discovered them when he crash-landed his plane on top of the tepuí in 1937, and they were not scientifically measured until 1949. The remoteness of the region and the dense jungle surrounding the falls mean that even today the best views are from the air.

The Angel Falls, Canaima National Park, Venezuela, plunges over the edge of a tepuí, or flat-topped mountain. Located in the Guiana Highlands, this awesome waterfall is 15 times the height of the Niagara Falls, making it the tallest free-flowing waterfall on the planet

WHITE SANDS

Over 700 square kilometres (270 square miles) of undulating, pure white sand occupies the northern end of the Chihuahuan Desert in New Mexico, making up the largest pure gypsum dune field in the world – the White Sands National Monument. Gypsum sands are incredibly beautiful and incredibly rare, requiring a combination of unique events to accumulate. Originally deposited 250 million years ago at the bottom of a shallow sea, the gypsum-baring rocks were exposed to the elements 70 million years ago when the uplift of the earth created a huge dome that would collapse to form the Tularosa Basin. Still ringed by mountains that are remnants of this original uplift, the Tularosa Basin has no drainage outlets, so all the gypsum dissolved by rainwater is deposited within the basin's walls. Most of the gypsum in the desert comes from a lake that dried out in the last Ice Age, but the ephemeral Lake Lucero continues to produce gypsum sand and glistening crystals year after year, enlarging the desert at a rate of 9 metres (30 feet) annually.

These type of dune at White Sands require a unique set of events to accumulate, and are extremely rare

THE ENCHANTED ISLES

Las Encantadas, meaning 'the enchanted', were named by the bishop of Panama, Tomás de Berlanga, whose ship drifted off course while en route to Peru in 1535. His later description of the giant tortoises (*galápagos* in Spanish) gave the islands another, now better-known name. These early sailors found the islands in much the same way as the animals and plants that make up the unique ecosystem – by chance. The chance arrival of a species of finch, hundreds of thousands of years ago, has led to what scientists term adaptive radiation, in its most extreme form. Thirteen species of finch have evolved from that one ancestral form, and this impressive example of evolution in progress was one of the many inspirations for the great scientific observer of the nineteenth century, Charles Darwin. His unique skill in observing and apparently explaining the unexplainable (the many varieties of finches), and ignoring the perhaps more obvious (gigantism in tortoises that were free from predation), led to a revolution in the biological sciences.

The volcanic landscape of Santiago Island, viewed from the shores of Bartolome Island. The unique plants and animals of the islands were the inspiration for Charles Darwin's theory on the origin of species

VOLCANOES OF THE DEEP

During the 1970s geologists had long suspected that volcanic activity on the sea floor might create the unusual conditions known as hydrothermal venting, but nobody thought that these inhospitable environments might also be oases of life. In 1977 a group of geologists made the outstanding biological discovery of the twentieth century: giant tube worms and clams growing on hydrothermal vents. It was such a surprise that they did not even have the equipment with them to preserve the animals they collected. When the biologists returned in 1979, they realized that these animals were not only completely new to science, but also relied on an energy source independent of the sun: bacteria that can use the chemicals in the vent fluid as food. The unusual nature of organisms at deep-sea vents has led many to suspect that vents may have played a role in the origin of life on earth, and perhaps on other planets.

The desert landscape of Monument Valley with the East Mitten formation in the foreground. The great buttes, mesas and spires rise suddenly out of the barren sands and are the result of erosion over the millennia

MONUMENT VALLEY

Despite its name, Monument Valley is not a valley in the true sense – it is a sprawling desert plain, coloured by the distinctive red sands of Utah and Arizona. Rivers meandered over the region 270 million years ago, depositing the sandstone, siltstone and shale that make up the valley we see today. It was the massive uplift and folding of the Colorado Plateau some 20 million years ago that initiated the creation of the iconic geological formations after which the valley is named. The buttes and mesas – flat-topped, isolated hills with steep sides – and spires that suddenly loom out of the level plain are the result of wind and water erosion acting on the different layers of rock that were deposited there over time before being haphazardly uplifted. The softer underlying shale layers are protected by the topmost siltstone layer; where there are gaps in this top layer the softer rock will erode rapidly, creating the formations that have inspired for centuries those lucky enough to have seen them.

The 'Ear of the Wind' formation in Monument Valley. Many of the formations in Monument Valley have evocative names given to them by the Navajo Indians who have lived in the area for centuries

The Giant Redwood, found
in the forests of the Sierra
Nevada mountains, California.
This is the largest species of
tree, and has been around
since the time of the
dinosaurs. It is highly
specialized and able
to survive forest fires
and plant diseases

ON THE SHOULDERS OF GIANTS

The slopes of the lofty Sierra Nevada Mountains are
home to a unique species of conifer, the giant redwood
(*Sequoiadendron giganteum*). The largest of trees, it
can grow to over 90 metres (295 feet) tall and 30
metres (100 feet) in circumference, yet the seed cone
is only the size of a hen's egg. These seeds, though
plentiful, take centuries to grow into the majestic
giants we see today. Thick bark allows the trees to
pass unscathed through forest fires that kill other
faster growing trees around them, while natural wood
preservatives protect them from disease. In fact, it is
not known how long a giant redwood can live for.
Trees felled long before their natural death have been
aged at 3,500 years – long enough to outlive a
civilization. The species itself has outlived the
dinosaurs.

This giant redwood, known
as 'General Sherman', is
found in Sequoia National
Park, California. At 275 feet
(84 metres) tall, 101 feet (31
metres) in circumference at
the base and 52,500 cubic
feet (1,487 cubic metres) in
volume, it is the largest
living tree in the world

LAND OF FIRE AND WATER

Established in 1872, Yellowstone Park in the United States was the world's first national park. Best known for its geyser, Old Faithful, that erupts every 33–120 minutes, the 8,983 square kilometres (3,465 square miles) of park is made up of broad volcanic plateaux containing 10,000 hot springs, geysers, mud cauldrons, hot rivers and steam vents. It is home to fossil forests, a mountain made of obsidian and the United States' largest mountain lake, Yellowstone Lake. The geothermal activity of Yellowstone is due to the chamber of partially molten magma that has been heating water that drains down through the rocks from the nearby mountains since the area formed over 600,000 years ago. The water bursts through the earth with such force that some geysers erupt 30 metres (100 feet) into the air, a constant reminder of the area's ongoing volcanism; two volcanic vents are also rising again, making Yellowstone Lake tilt slowly southward.

The eruption of Castle Geyser in Yellowstone National Park, Wyoming, occurs, on average, every 12.5 hours. Yellowstone Park is the world's first National Park and an area of ongoing volcanism characterized by hot springs, fumeroles and geysers

PAINTINGS IN THE SANDS

The multicoloured, barren areas – or 'badlands' – of the Painted Desert cover 19,400 square kilometres (7,490 square miles) and stretch 240 kilometres (150 miles) south-eastwards from the Grand Canyon along the Little Colorado River. More than just a region of arid desert sands, the shale and sandstone of the area come in myriad intense colours, with shades of white, yellow, red, blue and lavender banding the impressive buttes and huge mesas of the region. Within this rolling, technicolour terrain lie the petrified and preserved remains of 170 million-year-old trees. Like the stone and the sand of the surrounding desert, the fossilized forests are brilliantly coloured and form huge piles of giant logs strewn across the ground, creating one of the world's largest – and arguably most beautiful – petrified forests. Rich in fossils and archaeological history, the Painted Desert has a varied past. The Navajo tribe use the variegated sands in ceremonial paintings, and when the desert glows beneath a pink and purple haze such mysticism is easy to comprehend.

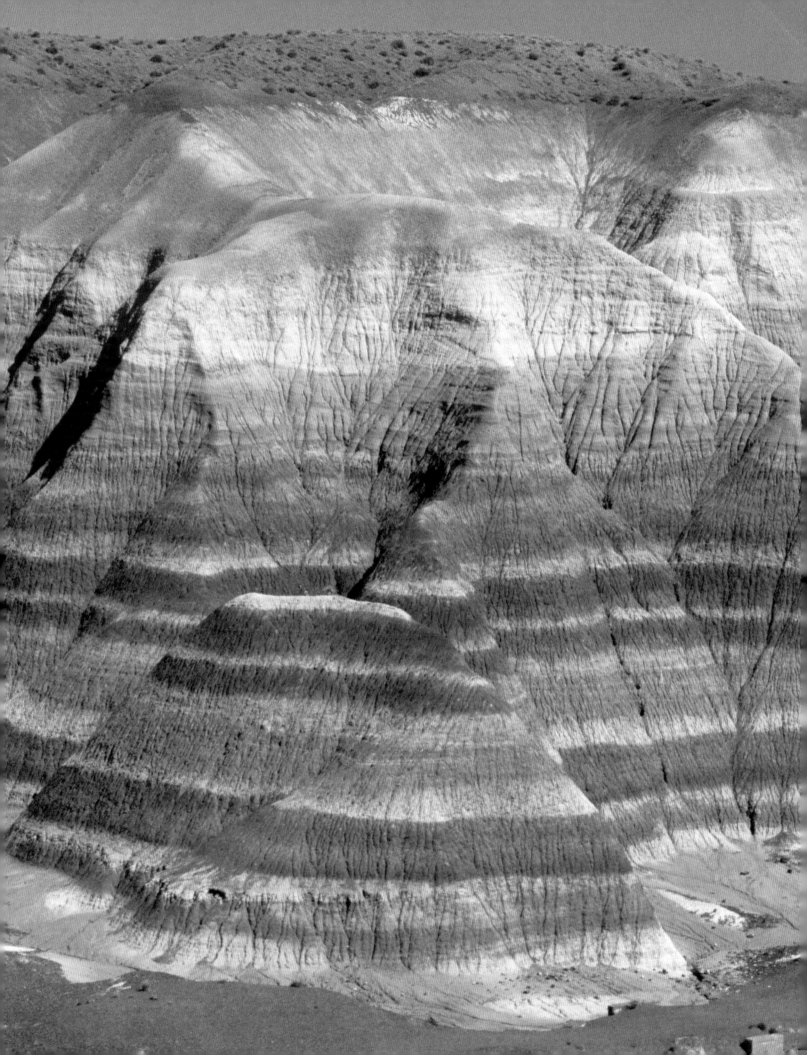

BAYS OF BAJA

The long and narrow peninsula of Baja, California stretches 1,220 kilometres (760 miles) south-west from the north-west corner of Mexico, separating the Gulf of California from the Pacific Ocean. Only 40 kilometres (25 miles) wide in some places, this rugged region ranges from 3,000-metre (9,845 feet) high granite mountains in the north, giving way first to volcanoes and then to lowlands, until finally rising again to over 2,000 metres (6,565 feet) at the very tip of the peninsula. The coastal lagoons and sheltered natural harbours of the Pacific coast are home to the most northerly Pacific mangrove forests, and are important wintering sites for grey whales and nesting grounds for endangered marine turtles. The hundreds of isolated islands of the gulf are home to rare birds and spectacular coves. The edge of one of the earth's continental plates cuts through the Gulf of California to the northern end of the Baja Peninsula, where it becomes known as the San Andreas Fault, which threatens to one day rend the whole peninsula away from the mainland.

A sandy cove on Isla San Francisco, just off the east coast of Baja California. The Baja peninsula is a volcanic and mountainous region whose surrounding islands and waters are a haven for wildlife

A dinosaur bone reveals itself in the sandstone of Dinosaur Provincial Park. Over 23,000 dinosaur fossils have been found here to date, representing every known group of dinosaurs from the Cretaceous period. Erosion continues to shape the rocks in the park and to expose more and more fossils

CRETACEOUS PARK

Dinosaur Provincial Park in the badlands of Alberta in Canada is an amazing place, a monument to the lost lands of the past. Fifteen thousand years ago the region lay beneath the thick ice that dominated the northern hemisphere during the last Ice Age. This 600-metre (1,970 feet) thick ice sheet carved the earth under it, its melt waters creating knife-edge channels that formed the basis for the incredible terrain seen there today. Wind and water made the badlands — dramatic valleys and eerie, isolated rock pillars called 'hoodoo' formations, so named because they call to mind the work of black magic. It is against this awesome backdrop that dinosaur fossils are found in abundance — creatures that last walked the earth 75 million years ago in the Cretaceous period. More than 23,000 dinosaur fossils have been found, including tyrannosaurs. In fact, specimens from every known group of dinosaurs from the Cretaceous period have been uncovered from this single location.

An isolated rock formation, or 'hoodoo' formation, stands amidst the badlands of Dinosaur Provincial Park. Wind and water have sculpted the terrain to produce eerie formations

The edge of the mighty Moreno Glacier, Los Glaciares National Park. Located in southwest Argentina, near to Upsala and Viedma Glaciers and south of the Fitzroy Massif, the Moreno glacier is thought to be the only glacier in the world that is not retreating

HOME OF THE CONDOR

In south-west Argentina the three mighty glaciers of Periot Moreno, Upsala and Viedma flow across a barren mountainscape, draining into Lakes Argentino and Viedma. North of them lies the great Fitzroy Massif, one of the greatest mountaineering challenges of our time. Named after the master of HMS *Beagle*, the British survey ship that was Charles Darwin's home during his voyages, this peak has become what some climbers call the ultimate mountain. Although small compared to the giants of the Himalaya, to climb it requires the skills of both a rock and ice climber. Remarkably, it was first climbed in 1952 by the French team of Lionel Terray and Guido Magnone. Today, some seasons go by with barely an ascent on the mountain, although trekkers from around the world frequent the region, hoping to visit the giant Moreno glacier, thought to be the only non-retreating glacier in the world.

The Fitzroy Massif and Cerro Torre mountains of Los Glaciares National Park. These jagged peaks may not be as big as the mountains in the Himalayas, but they are some of the world's toughest mountains to climb

LAKE SUPERIOR

Formed by the action of the Laurentian ice sheet that
retreated at the end of the last Ice Age, Lake Superior
is the largest freshwater lake, by area, in the world.
The huge lake basin, carved out of granite bedrock, is
616 kilometres (380 miles) long and 258 kilometres
(160 miles) wide, with a surface area of 82,100 square
kilometres (31,670 square miles). It is the most north-
westerly of all the Great Lakes of North America, with
its 4,393 kilometres (2,730 miles) of shoreline falling
within the territories of Ontario in Canada and
Michigan, Minnesota and Wisconsin in the United
States. It is also the deepest, with a maximum depth
of 406 metres (1,335 feet). This huge body of water is
fed by 200 rivers and then empties into Lake Huron.
The water of Lake Superior, 99 per cent of which is
believed to be of glacial origin, is also the coldest of
all the Great Lakes. It is so cold and deep that the lake
is rumoured to never give up its dead – the bodies that
sink beneath its surface are never seen again.

LAKES FROM MARS

Laguna Verde lies high in the Bolivian Andes in a region known as the Altiplano, or high plains. This bleak land of volcanoes, sulphurous steam vents and brightly tinted lakes is thought to be similar to areas on the planet Mars, where water may have once existed. NASA has focused a programme here to investigate life in extreme environments in the hope that one day we might understand trace fossils from ancient Martian lakes. It is no surprise that the bright green waters are rich in cyanobacteria, and in neighbouring Laguna Blanca, stromatolites — layers of limestone formed by bacteria — have been discovered on the lake bed. The diatoms (algae) of the lakes are subjected to extreme levels of UV radiation, and have evolved unique shielding strategies to prevent them from damage. On the summit of the volcano Licancabur lies the highest lake in the world; despite temperatures of -30°C (-22°F) at an altitude of 5,916 metres (19,410 feet), the water is kept from freezing by volcanic heat.

Laguna Verde, in the middle distance, lies within the volcanic landscape of the Altiplano in the Bolivian Andes. Environments here are thought to be comparable with those of Mars

PLUNGING WATER

The dark interior of Guyana has held the promise of treasure for centuries. In 1595 Sir Walter Raleigh was the first European to explore the region in search of the legendary city of El Dorado. He found gold and diamonds, but the real treasures of Guyana are its virgin rainforests, running all the way from the mangrove swamps of the coast to the high Guianan Shield Plateau, and the amazing organisms and river systems found within them. In the depths of the jungle, where the Potaro River plunges over the side of the Pakaraima Plateau, are the magnificent Kaieteur Falls. A wall of water, 100 metres (330 feet) wide, plummets 226 metres (745 feet) in a single drop – the world's largest single drop waterfall. The falls continue to descend another 25 metres (80 feet) through a tree-covered gorge, 8 kilometres (5 miles) long and home to the timorous cock-of-the-rock. The vast sandstone shelf, over which the falls tumble, provides nesting places for the makanaima swifts that can be seen in rapid flight above the crashing water.

Deep inside the interior of Guyana, within one of the world's least disturbed rainforests, the Kaieteur Falls' unique dimensions make it the world's largest single drop waterfall

HAWAIIAN SHIELD

Some 5 kilometres (3 miles) below the surface of the tropical Pacific, the flanks of the world's largest single object rise up from the deep abyssal plain. The island of Hawaii is no mere atoll; it is the world's largest shield volcano – a wide, spreading volcano that gets it shape from the fluid nature of its lava. Its enormous weight compresses the sea floor it rests on to the depth of some 8 kilometres (5 miles), which means that the total height of the volcano itself is nearly 17 kilometres (10 miles), over 8 kilometres (5 miles) higher than Mount Everest. The other main peaks of Hawaii – Mauna Loa and Mauna Kea – lie dormant, but at Kilauea, rivers of lava pour down the mountain from the main vent at Pu'u O'o, forming new land as they flow into the Pacific Ocean. The barren desert-like extinct lava fields are soon colonized by native Hawaiian plant life, and a national park has been created on Hawaii to protect these unusual habitats – and the unwary tourist from the powerful geology.

The main Pu'u O'o vent of Kilauea volcano erupts. Kilauea is the only active volcano on Hawaii and the site of the world's longest continuous eruption, rivering lava down the mountainside into the sea since 1983

WORLD OF WHITE AND BLUE

The Salar de Uyuni is a geological marvel high in the Bolivian Altiplano. A vast plateau that separates the mountainous part of Bolivia from the steamy Amazonian Basin, the Altiplano is the ultimate in big sky, barren, harsh environments. Transport an unsuspecting visitor to the middle of the Salar and they might think they were on another planet. It is a vista of sheer white salt that stretches for 12,000 square miles (4,635 square miles), intercepted only by the occasional 'island' – rocky outcrops that show the level of the ancient Lake Minchin from which the Salar formed some 40,000 years ago. This is the largest salt flat on the planet and it contains an estimated 10 billion tonnes of salt – enough to supply the world for 50 years. In November the wet season brings three species of flamingo here to breed; the rest of the year tourists drive at speed across the flats, spending the night at a hotel made entirely from salt.

The vast salt-flats of the Salar de Uyuni contain 10 billion tonnes of salt. This region, high in the Bolivian Altiplano, separates the Bolivian Andes from the Amazon Basin and is a beautiful, but barren, environment

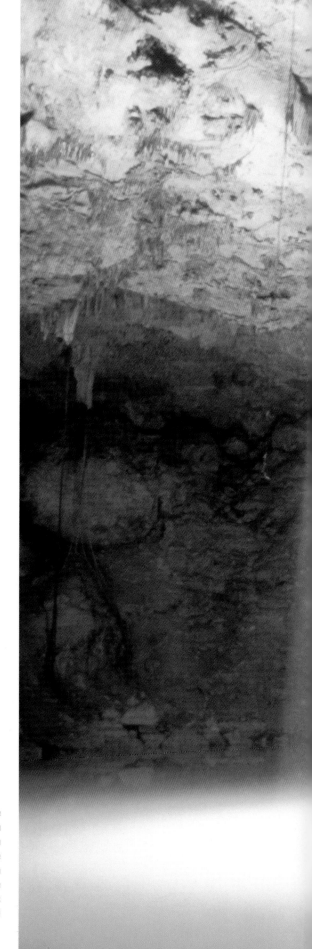

SACRIFICIAL WELLS

The Yucatán Peninsula of Mexico is almost bereft of surface water; its rainfall is simply absorbed by the highly porous limestone bedrock of the region. The acid nature of the water dissolves the underlying layers of soft rock and, over time, creates water-filled underground caverns, or cenotes. Derived from the Mayan word *dzonot*, meaning 'cavity of water', these caves were the Maya people's main source of fresh water in the jungle. Some are barely accessible, hidden deep within subterranean passages, like X'Keken. A tranquil place, X'Keken is 45 metres (150 feet) in diameter, with fish flitting through its cool, crystalline waters and stalactites illuminated by the single shaft of light that penetrates the arched roof. Other caves whose roofs have collapsed form natural wells around which great civilizations have arisen. The famed Mayan city of Chichén Itzá is such a place; it is here that the Cenote of Sacrifice is found, full of Mayan offerings of gold and jade linked to human sacrifice.

The cenote X'Keken is one of the many subterranean caverns of the Yucatán Peninsula. They were important to the Maya as a source for water and were believed to be gateways to the underworld

COOL DESERT SANDS

Lying in the shadow of two mountain ranges and sucked dry by cold water currents from the Antarctic, some parts of the Atacama Desert have not had rain for centuries. It is the driest place on earth, but unlike other deserts, it is not a place of searing heat as average summer temperatures are just 19°C (66.2°F). The Atacama is rich in salts, especially sodium nitrate, that pile up at the bases of the mountains that hem it. A coastal range separates the desert from the Pacific Ocean to the west, while to the east Andean volcanoes mark the Argentinean frontier. This narrow, 1,000-kilometre (620 miles) long strip of northern Chile is thought to be the oldest desert in the world, between 10 and 15 million years old; its driest regions do not sustain any kind of life. Even cyanobacteria, which can live under rocks, cannot carve out an existence in this most extreme of environments.

The Valley of the Moon in the Atacama Desert is the driest place on earth. Hemmed in by mountains, the desert is especially valuable for its mineral salts

THE AMAZON RIVER

The course of the River Amazon begins in the Andes, just 160 kilometres (100 miles) from the Pacific Ocean and then meanders eastwards for 6,400 kilometres (3,980 miles) until it reaches the Atlantic. Almost splitting South America in two and flowing through spectacular scenery, the Amazon is the largest drainage system in the world; at its mouth it is a staggering 64 kilometres (40 miles) wide and the fresh water it pours into the Atlantic dilutes the salt water within 150 kilometres (95 miles) of the shore. Within the Amazon River Basin is the Amazon rainforest, home to trees so tall they require enormous buttress roots to stabilize them. The river and its tributaries are full of fascinating species such as anacondas, electric fish, piranha, the giant arapaima fish, river dolphins, manatees and caimans. The surrounding forests are also teeming with life: vampire bats, jaguars, sloths, monkeys and many more live here in the region that contains half of the world's remaining rainforest.

The waters of the Amazon, and those of its equally mighty tributaries such as the Rio Negro, can flood in the rainy season to engulf surrounding forests in as much as 40 metres (130 feet) of water

LAND OF THE GIANTS

Where the Cuiaba and Paraguay Rivers meet, the greatest wetland ecosystem on the planet is formed. During the wet season, flooding across the Pantanal region can extend over 200,000 square kilometres (77,220 square miles), and the enormous plain is covered by up to several metres of water. In May the waters ebb and a layer of fine humus is left in the soil, greatly enriching it. This rich alluvial plain is home to an astonishing variety of plant life, including everything from thick forest to floating islands of river vegetation, or *baías*, and giant waterlilies that can support the weight of a small person. At least 80 species of mammal, 650 bird species and 50 species of reptile have been recorded here, including the endangered jaguar, marsh deer and giant anteater. The world's largest parrot, the giant hyacinth macaw, is from this region, although its population has shrunk as humans have moved in.

A huge alluvial plain that occurs at the confluence of the Cuiaba and Paraguay Rivers, the Pantanal region of Brazil is the world's greatest wetland ecosystem, and home to giant water lillies

EXPLOSION OF LIFE

It may seem surprising, but the beautiful Canadian Rockies, North Wales (in the United Kingdom) and China's Yunnan Province all have something in common – their age. At these sites, rocks can be dated to a period known as the Cambrian, from the Latin word for Wales, where British geologists first recorded the great stratigraphy of life. It was Charles Walcott, the American palaeontologist, who first discovered the remarkable soft-bodied fossil deposits in the Canadian Rockies' Burgess Pass in 1909. In the century that followed, experts reconstructed the organisms from this 500 million-year-old mud slide to uncover something remarkable: the first recorded flourishing of large animal life on the planet, in the shallow seas of the Cambrian. The deposits yielded nearly all the major animal groups we know today, including chordates (species with primitive vertebrae), and many other unusual forms that have since died out. However, it was not until 1984 that evidence for this Cambrian explosion of life was confirmed by the discovery of similar fossils, dated to the same period, in Yunnan, China.

Mount Proboscis is only one of many equally spectacular peaks found throughout the Canadian Rockies. The ranges are made from rocks that date to the Cambrian period, some 490 million years ago, where life on earth 'exploded' in to a dazzling array of bizarre forms

Although it is now extinct, the devastating birth, and subsequent nine years of eruption, of Paricutín changed Mexico forever. The ash of the volcano covered many miles, and the lava flows engulfed nearby villages, including the volcano's namesake, Paricutín

YOUTHFUL FIRE

Although we think of the landscape as being formed over the course of millennia and do not expect it to change noticeably in our lifetime, the world's youngest volcano was born as recently as 20 February 1943 in Mexico. As local farmers tended their crops in a cornfield, the ground beneath them fissured and a vent opened, spewing forth a sulphurous mass of lava and gas that fell as cinders all around. This was the beginning of a cinder cone that reached 335 metres (1,100 feet) in height in just one year. Paricutín, named after one of the villages it engulfed, continued to erupt and grow as lava flowed done its sides for eight more years. In 1952 it died, having grown to 425 metres (1,400 feet) high and covering over 150 square kilometres (60 square miles) of land in ash. Paricutín is a monogenetic volcano with only a single, nine-year eruption that created a natural wonder of the modern world – the birth of a mountain.

Paricutín is the world's youngest volcano. It was born as recently as 1943, when it grew rapidly and violently out of the flat land around it

EMERALD CAVES

The muted light of the sun forcing its way through the lush, dense canopy of the tropical jungle and then deep into the underground Río Camuy cave system throws into relief the incredible karst formations of this subterranean wonder. Found deep within the rainforests of northern Puerto Rico, the region's many sinkholes and caverns make up the third largest cave system in the world. Carved out by the Camuy River over 1 million years ago, very little of the system has been explored, but already it is being hailed as a natural masterpiece. The largest cavern is the cathedral-like Cueva Clara, 210 metres (690 feet) long and 65 metres (215 feet) high; the sinkhole Tres Pueblos is equally jaw-dropping at 215 metres (705 feet) wide and 130 metres (430 feet) deep. This exquisite underworld, a portal to Puerto Rico's hidden depths, is home to more than just spectacular stalactites; a unique species of blind fish makes its home there.

A network of caves exists underneath the tropical jungle of northwest Puerto Rico. The Río Camuy cave system is the third largest in the world. Most of the caves and sinkholes are unexplored

YOSEMITE

In the western United States, the mighty Sierra Nevada mountain range has given rise to one of the great natural wonders of the world: Yosemite Valley and the high country surrounding it. Much of the region is recently uplifted granite, and the valley is famous for its remarkable glacial land forms, a relic from the last ice ages of the Pleistocene era. The most spectacular cliff in perhaps all of the United States is El Capitan, a huge granitic monolith that guards the valley and provides the most spectacular climbing routes in the country. Contrary to popular belief, the mountain of Half Dome was created by the erosion of fault lines, not the movement of past glaciers, although evidence of them is widespread in other areas. Yosemite's awesome geology is matched by a unique biology – giant redwood trees are widespread in the valleys, while brown bears, mule deer and bobcats provide photo opportunities for the tourists.

PIRATE
CAVE

A one-time haven for pirates and buccaneers, the extensive reefs and cayes – or islets – of Belize still retain their aura of adventure and mystery. The world's second largest barrier reef was formed when the sea rose at the end of the last Ice Age and flooded the local karst cave systems. This underwater realm lures divers with the promise of sinkholes, like the Blue Hole, 305 metres (1,000 feet) in diameter and dropping 123 metres (400 feet) into the depths. Among the coral reefs, over 450 cayes fringed with mangrove forest and coconut groves dot the exquisitely clear, blue waters of the Atlantic-Caribbean coast, and living among this tropical paradise are the shy and ponderous manatees, American crocodiles, logger-head turtles and schools of sharks. The beauty and bounty of Belize's waters have attracted humans for 2,500 years, from the Mayan fishing communities to today's divers in search of an underwater paradise.

The Blue Hole of Belize is an almost perfectly circular sinkhole. It is part of the extensive karst cave system that is now submerged beneath the tropical waters of the Atlantic-Caribbean coast. The region is home to the world's second largest barrier reef

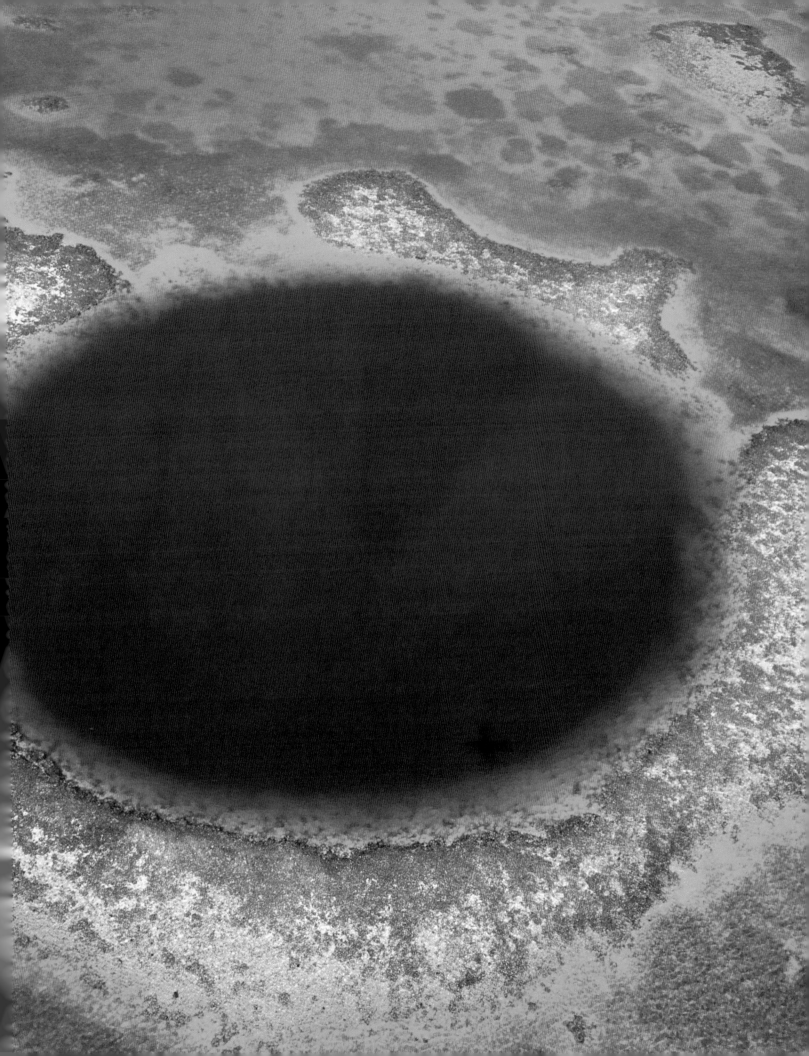

TREELESS PLAINS

In the far northern latitudes of the coldest of all the earth's biomes – an area characterized by the interdependent organisms inhabiting the region – is the Arctic Tundra. Derived from the Finnish word *tunturia*, meaning 'treeless plains', the tundra's characteristic frosted landscapes and low temperatures shape much of Canada, Alaska and Siberia. Low rainfall and a short growing season limit plant life to shrubs, sedges, mosses and grasses. Winter temperatures average -34°C (-29ºF), and in summer barely make it above freezing. The constant freezing creates a deep layer of frozen soil and gravel – permafrost – that blocks the growth of plant roots. This barren land is one of rare beauty, and despite limited food is home to a diverse range of mammal species, including lemmings, arctic hares, arctic foxes and polar bears. Animals are adapted to the long, cold winters, breeding and raising young quickly during the brief summer months.

This tundra of Alaska in autumn is representative of tundra ecosystems across the far northern latitudes. These barren and beautiful landscapes are characterized by the lack of trees and by sedges, mosses and grasses that can survive the extreme cold

The Bay of Fundy is characterized by massive erosion caused by the powerful tidal forces of the region. The tides carry with them huge amounts of coastal red sandstone and carve rock formations like this one at Shepody Bay

TIDE OF TIDES

The Bay of Fundy is the earth's superlative example of tidal power, and one of the seven natural wonders of the world. Running 280 kilometres (175 miles) inland between the Canadian provinces of New Brunswick and Nova Scotia, this ocean inlet, encircled by steep bedrock cliffs, has the highest tides in the world, reaching up to 21 metres (70 feet). As the bay narrows, the effects of these extraordinary natural forces are intensified. The influx of water as the tide rises causes the rapids in St John's River to flow backwards, creating the incredible phenomenon of waterfalls flowing in reverse. The Petitcodiac River witnesses tides that rise at a rate of 3 metres (10 feet) per hour — a tidal surge that results in 2-metre (7 feet) high tidal bores (fast-flowing waves that run upstream). A staggering 100 billion tonnes of water empty in and out of the bay every day.

Crater Lake in Oregon is the water-filled remnant of Mount Mazama which erupted, and collapsed, in 4860 BC. Geological activity continues in the area; Wizard Island (pictured) is a cinder cone that has grown up from the caldera floor

RELIC OF THE UNDERWORLD

Beneath the calm, blue waters of Crater Lake, geothermal heat can still be detected, testament to the power of the eruption that created this spectacular land form. The lake is in the collapsed caldera of Mount Mazama, a 4,000-metre (13,125 feet) high mountain that once stood here. In 4860 BC the mountain catastrophically erupted, sending pumice and ash over 10 kilometres (6 miles) into the sky, and super-heated pyroclastic flows over 60 kilometres (35 miles) in distance. Local Klamath Indians undoubtedly witnessed this event; legends tell of a battle between Lloa, god of the underworld, and his rival Skell, the sky god. Archaeological excavations have uncovered sagebrush sandals baked and charred with mud from the eruption. As the eruption continued, the caldera collapsed, and over hundreds of years filled with water to form the lake. Smaller eruptions from the caldera floor formed cinder cones, some of which are visible at the surface, such as Wizard Island.

THE GREAT DIVIDE

In the western part of Peru, where the Rio Santa drains to the Pacific and the Rio Marañon to the Atlantic, a great mountain range exists, known locally as the Cordillera Blanca. The most extensive tropical mountain range in the world, its summit is the peak of Nevado Huascarán, 6,768 metres (22,200 feet) in height. An astonishing 722 individual glaciers drain from this area, covering an area of over 700 square kilometres (270 square miles). Mountaineers flock here to the great peaks, such as Alpamayo and Huascarán, reachable only by technical rock and ice routes. Within the park 10 unique mammal species can be found, including the spectacled bear and the vicuña. Despite the inhospitable environment, including frequent deadly rock and ice avalanches, over two centuries of human occupation has been recorded here.

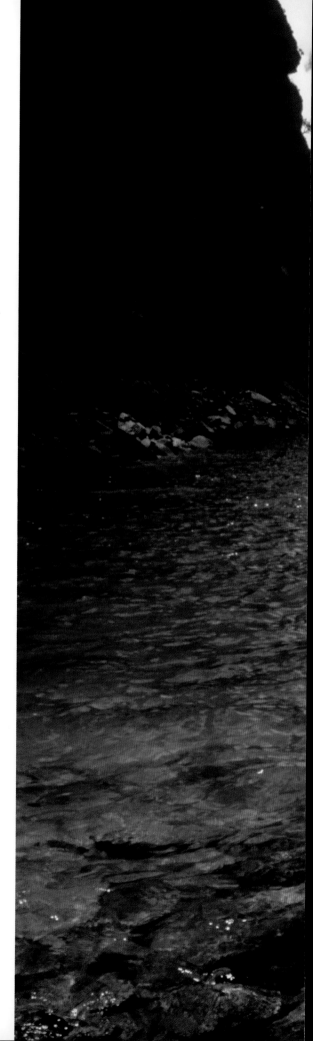

Lago Paron in the Huascarán National Park lies against the spectacular backdrop of the Cordillera Blanca mountain range. The region is drained by 722 different glaciers. Unique mammals are found here, including the spectacled bear and the vicuña

Isla del Coco, or Cocos Island, and the surrounding cays, are off the coast of Costa Rica, in the Pacific Ocean. The only island to support tropical rainforest and montane cloud forest in the eastern tropical Pacific, Cocos Island is a truly remote island paradise

SHARK PARADISE

A mountain range stretches from Costa Rica to the Galápagos Archipelago, almost completely submerged by the waters of the Pacific Ocean. Only one summit penetrates the ocean surface: the rugged and mountainous Isla del Cocos, 550 kilometres (340 miles) off the coast of Costa Rica. Waterfalls plunge over the vertical cliffs that rise 200 metres (655 feet) out of the sea, draining the lush mountains of the island's interior. Isla del Coco is the only island of the eastern tropical Pacific to support tropical rainforest and montane cloud forest. Its high relief (634 metres, or 2,080 feet) promotes around 7,000 millimetres (275 inches) of precipitation annually, encouraging exuberant growth in the island's plant life. Offshore is the most extensive coral reef in the south-east Pacific, creating an incredibly rich marine environment. The region is particularly known for pelagic sharks (those that prefer open seas and waters) and rays, that gather there in large numbers, but the inland forests and reef environments contribute to the outstanding beauty of this remote island paradise.

The waters around the Isla del Coco are a natural habitat for white-finned sharks, as well as gigantic hammerhead sharks, tuna, parrot fish, manta rays, and marine turtles

THE HIGH ONE

The highest mountain in North America at 6,194 metres (20,325 feet), Denali in Alaska is a place of extremes. Officially named Mount McKinley, the local Athabascan name *Denali*, meaning 'the high one', is a fitting moniker that is now more commonly used. A granite monolith rising out of glacier-covered sedimentary plains, the twin peaks of Denali have the greatest vertical relief of any mountain in the world, and it continues to grow 1 millimetre ($^1/_{16}$ inch) per year. Only 160 kilometres (100 miles) outside the Arctic Circle, Denali is thought to be the coldest mountain in the world. The combination of its location with the wind chill factors caused by the channelling of jet stream winds through narrow gullies lead to temperatures that plummet far enough below zero to flash freeze climbers on its slopes. Add to this the problem of reduced air pressure in high latitudes, making altitude acclimatization difficult, and it becomes apparent that Denali is one of the world's most hostile mountains, and worthy of the respect given to it by mountaineers across the globe.

Mount McKinley or *Denali*,
as it is named in the
local Athabascan language,
is the highest mountain
in North America

THE DEVIL'S THROAT

Straddling the border between Argentina and Brazil is one of the world's great waterfalls – the Iguaçu Falls. In the local Guaraní Indian language, the name means 'great water', which the falls certainly live up to. The falls are found where the Iguaçu River drops off the Paraná Plateau, 14 kilometres (10 miles) upstream of its confluence with the Upper Paraná River. The falls comprise 275 separate waterfalls plunging 80 metres (265 feet) over a horse-shoe shaped ledge some 2.7 kilometres (2 miles) wide. The rate of water flowing over the edge is, on average, twice that of the Victoria Falls in Africa and can reach more than 10 times that (12,750 cubic metres, or 450,265 cubic feet per second) in the rainy season. Despite the overall width, most of the water volume is concentrated on falls that tumble into a narrow chasm known as *Garganta do Diablo*, meaning 'devil's throat'. From the bottom of the falls a mist rises 500 metres (1,640 feet) into the air, shot through with rainbows – the delicate aftermath of this mighty fall.

The Iguaçu Falls straddle the border between Argentina and Brazil, where the Iguaçu River drops off the Paraná Plateau. The water tumbles over the falls and plunges into a narrow chasm known locally as the 'Devil's Throat'

ASIA AND AUSTRALASIA

The collision of India with the Eurasian landmass some 50 million years ago initiated the creation of the Asia we know today, together with a major climatic change that was to affect the entire world. As the Indian subcontinent pushed northwards into Eurasia, the Tibetan Plateau was thrust upwards. This huge mountain range, which includes the Himalaya and the highest peaks in the world, is still being formed; it is also growing faster than time and weather can erode it.

Asia has the longest coastline in the world, and its many islands and regions hemmed in by mountains provide ample opportunity for extraordinary biodiversity in the world. It has the region of highest marine biodiversity, an incredible number of biodiversity hotspots in Indonesia and the Philippines, and was host to the greatest volcanic explosion ever recorded – the stunning blast that was Tambora erupting in 1815. It stretches from the Dead Sea, some 400 metres (1,315 metres) below sea level, to the top of Mount Everest, 8,850 metres (29,035 feet) above sea level. Its natural wonders exist against a foreground of political instability, reflecting the ancient cultures that have survived side by side for millennia. It was the birthplace of civilization, and all major religions in the world today have their origins in Asia.

To the early European explorers, Australia and New Zealand represented the ends of the earth. The existence of a 'terra australis incognita', or the unknown southern land, had been debated long before the great exploratory expeditions of the fifteenth and sixteenth centuries. Australia and New Zealand have very different geologies. New Zealand lies along active fault lines, ensuring that its islands are mountainous regions of incredible volcanism. Australia, however, has rock surfaces that have been exposed to weathering for millions of years, and is a region of low relief and incredible rock formations. Australia and New Zealand share one thing that ensures they are full of natural wonders – isolation. The break-up of the supercontinent Gondwana some 150 million years ago and the spreading of the sea floor have meant that the native flora and fauna of Australasia have evolved independently for an incredibly long time, resulting in the unique marsupials of Australia and the diversity of birds and insects in New Zealand.

BAY OF THE DESCENDING
DRAGON

Some 3,000 islands in the Gulf of Bac Bo form the stunning seascape that is Ha Long Bay. Local legends describe how a giant dragon stomped on the earth with such force that valleys and mountains were created; when the valleys were flooded, the mountain tops became the pillars that rise vertically out of the water. Geological theory might dispute this — the pillars are undoubtedly the result of the processes of karst formation — but the beauty of this natural wonder is beyond doubt. Archaeological evidence indicates that these islands have in fact been used by humans for thousands of years — stone artefacts dating to 13,000 years ago indicate a flourishing culture in this region. The area is also biologically important, and the unique cave ecosystems are home to protected species. The bay is now protected under National Park and UNESCO World Heritage status.

These famous limestone pillars of Ha Long Bay form an archipelago of 3,000 islands, with unique species of plants and animals recorded from numerous cave systems

Mists hanging over the tropical rainforests of Sumatera Utara Province, Sumatra. This island was once entirely covered by rainforest, today only remnants of this remain. The forests are incredibly rich in biodiversity, with over 10,000 species of plant recorded

ISLAND OF THE ORANG-UTAN

The Indonesian island of Sumatra was once a vast expanse of rainforest, but today only remnants of this primeval jungle exist — the unforgivable result of human impact over the last 50 years. Despite this dramatic destruction of habitat, the rainforests of Sumatra are still places of incredible beauty and extreme natural importance. With the highest biodiversity in insular South-east Asia — 10,000 plant species, over 200 mammal species and 580 species of birds, many of which are only found on Sumatra — the 2.5 million hectare (6.1 million acres) region is burgeoning with life. The forests are home to the Sumatran orang-utan, the ponderous great ape of Asia, as well as tigers, elephants, tapirs, rhinoceros and the secretive sunbear. The eerie echoes of gibbon song pervade the lush vegetation, and all this is thrown into spectacular juxtaposition with Indonesia's highest volcano, the 3,800-metre (12,465 feet) high Gunung Kerinchi.

ABODE OF SNOW

The great mountain system of Asia, the Himalaya, forms one of the greatest geological barriers on the planet – the Tibetan Plateau to the north and the alluvial plains of India to the south. The ancient pilgrims of India coined the Sanskrit name *himalaya*, meaning 'abode of snow'; today these mountains are a lure to mountaineers and trekkers the world over. Connected to Mount Everest by the infamous South Col, the Lhotse-Nuptse Massif, the fourth highest mountain in the world, remains in Everest's shadow. Nuptse was first climbed in 1961 by a British expedition, and Lhotse – one of the world's few 8,000-metre (26,245 feet) peaks – by a Swiss team in 1956 just three years after the British success on Everest. The summit is crowned by numerous smaller peaks, the most difficult being Nuptse East, which was only climbed in 2003.

The moon rising above Nuptse and Lobuche, Khumbu Region, Nepalese Himalaya. The great mountains of Asia, the Himalaya, join the plains of India to the Tibetan Plateau, forming an awe-inspiring barrier of icy peaks

MOUNTAINS
OF MAGIC AND MYSTERY

The Chinese poets of ancient times referred to Guilin in Guangxi Province as a fairyland, with its great towers of rock rising from subtropical wetlands and immense caves with interiors carved into diabolical forms. Landscape artists were inspired to produce some of China's greatest art. Geologists today recognize this region as a prime example of tower karst – peaks of limestone left by the steady erosion of rainwater over the centuries. This area has been home to humans for more than 30,000 years, and prehistoric remains occupy many of the caves. The Lijang River and the enormous water supplies of the karst have allowed a great city to flourish here since the Sui and Tang dynasties beginning in the sixth century. Today, thousands of tourists travel to Guilin to marvel at the calming wonder of peaks and paddy fields.

Fishing on the Lijang River, Guilin. The Guilin area is home to great limestone karst mountain ranges, arising from sub-tropical wetlands, and has been heavily influenced by the last 30,000 years of human occupation

REAWAKENING THE
KRAKEN

Krakatoa is a name synonymous with disaster. The massive eruption of this volcanic island in 1883 was the second largest the world had ever seen. It plunged the Sunda Straits into darkness for nearly 24 hours, destroyed two-thirds of the island, caused 40-metre (130 feet) high tsunamis to decimate the Indonesian coastline and spewed ash 50 kilometres (30 miles) into the stratosphere, affecting the world's sunsets for three years. Krakatoa's destructive power sterilized the nearby islands of all life. Such events make even the remnants of the original island a terrible but wondrous monument to the power of the earth. Nature has reclaimed the barren islands, restoring the lush paradise, but Krakatoa leaves another legacy. Since that cataclysmic event it has not lain silent. The old volcano may have collapsed into the sea, but in its place is another – in 1927, Anak Krakatoa (meaning the 'child of Krakatoa') started to grow from the seabed and the ominous rumblings of Anak Krakatoa are a constant reminder of the past.

Anak Krakatoa erupting in Ujong Kulon National Park, Java, Indonesia. The eruption of Krakatoa in 1883 was the second greatest the world has ever seen. Anak Krakatoa still rumbles, a reminder of the volcanic power of this region

THE SAVAGE MOUNTAIN

K2 is named after a simple surveyor's symbol made in 1856 by T. G. Montgomerie during the Great Trigonometric Survey of India – it was merely the second peak in the Karakoram Range in Pakistan. The name has stuck, though it does nothing to reflect the magnificent and terrible beauty of this mountain. At 8,611 metres (28,250 metres), K2 is the second highest mountain in the world, but is thought by many to be the hardest mountain to climb, and one of the deadliest. Although attempts were made to reach the summit from 1902 onwards, it was not until 1954 that it was conquered by the Italian climbers Achille Compagnoni and Lino Lacedelli. Compared to Mount Everest, K2 is colder, the routes to the top are steeper and more challenging, and the weather is far less predictable. Its difficulty lures climbers from across the world, many to their deaths – over a quarter of those who make the summit die on the descent.

A party of mountaineers at Concordia, the meeting point of the great glaciers of the Karakoram. In the background, the awesome pyramid of K2 rises

HEAVENLY MOUNTAINS

In Central Asia on the border of Kyrgyzstan and China's Xinjiang Province lies the most beautiful mountain in the world – Khan Tengri. First mentioned in Chinese chronicles 1,200 years ago, it was not until 1931 that it was first climbed by the intrepid Ukrainian Alpinist M. T. Pogrebetskiy. Khan Tengri lies at the heart of the great Tian Shan mountain range, meaning 'heavenly mountains', which extends for nearly 2,500 kilometres (1,550 miles) and has glaciers over 70 kilometres (40 miles) in length. The highest mountain in the range is Pik Pobeda at 7,439 metres (24,400 feet); Khan Tengri is slightly lower at 7,010 metres (23,000 feet), if you include the mushroom of snow at the summit. Adventurers have been lured here for centuries – the mountain is visible from the ancient Silk Road, the trade route that linked China with the west. Today mountaineers scale its peak via difficult rock and ice routes.

Low clouds hang over the Tien Shan region. This Central Asian mountain range is one of the most remote and spectacular in the world

RIVER DEEP, MOUNTAIN HIGH

The Yangtze is Asia's longest river and the world's third longest and most voluminous river. Known to the Chinese as *Ch'ang Chiang*, meaning 'long river', it winds for 6,300 kilometres (3,915 miles) from the Tibetan Plateau to the East China Sea. Over three-quarters of the river runs through mountainous terrain. During the course of its flow, it comes within 50 kilometres (30 miles) of China's other great rivers, the Mekong and the Salween, running parallel with them for 400 kilometres (240 miles) through China's most biodiverse region. The Yangtze passes through the Three Gorges, the most treacherous section of the watercourse. Here the river narrows and deepens to over 150 metres (490 feet), making it the world's deepest river; staggering 600-metre (1,970 feet) high gorges line its path. At its mouth the river empties 31,152,000 litres (8,229,485 gallons) of water per second into the sea – a true indication of the enduring power of the river that sustains a third of China's burgeoning population.

Wu Gorge, one of the Three Gorges on the Yangtze River. This, the world's third longest river, passes through some of the most dramatic scenery on earth

Daylight makes ghostly shadows in the enormous Sarawak chamber in the Good Luck cave, one of the many caves in the Gunung Mulu region. It is the largest rock chamber in the world

CAVE OF GOOD LUCK

In northern Sarawak on the island of Borneo, a fantastical cave system exists beneath a land of tropical forest, mountains, waterfalls and hot springs. Within the boundaries of the Gunung Mulu National Park, nature is at its most exuberant. The region contains many organisms that are found nowhere else in the world, and is also home to the world's smallest mammal, the 2-gram (0.06 oz) Savi pygmy shrew. The great limestone Gunung Massif dominates the mountain ranges, rising to 2,377 metres (7,800 feet), but it is the caves beneath the land that make this region so special. Created by rivers eroding rocks that were uplifted over 2 million years ago, these caves are sacred to local people and home to the largest colonies of cave-dwelling swifts in the world. Deer Cave, an ancient burial ground, is the world's largest natural cave passage, and the Good Luck Cave contains the world's largest cave chamber, measuring 600 metres (1,970 feet) long, 415 metres (1,360 feet) wide and 80 metres (260 feet) high.

The limestone peaks of Gunung Mulu National Park have been eroded into knife-edge ridges by the action of rain. The combination of jungle and razor-sharp rocks makes this region almost impenetrable

Cherry tree branches frame this view of Mount Fuji, near Yamanashi. The snow-capped peak is a focal point for Japanese culture and spiritual belief; every year many thousands of people trek to the summit during the warm summer months

MOUNTAIN
OF EVERLASTING LIFE

Sacred to the Japanese and iconic the world over, Mount Fuji is the highest of all Japan's volcanoes. At 3,776 metres (12,390 feet) high and characteristically snow-capped, its seemingly perfect cone-shaped profile belies the fact that Mount Fuji is actually a complex of several volcanoes. The largest and most recent of these, Shin Fuji, has erupted over the last 10,000 years to subsume the profiles of the other volcanoes around it into one large mountain measuring 50 kilometres (30 miles) in diameter at the base. Its last recorded eruption was in 1707, but scientists do not consider the volcano to be extinct. Nor is it any less alive to the Japanese populace, being a focus of religious and spiritual belief. Until a little over a hundred years ago, women were forbidden to climb the peak, and reaching the summit was the province of pilgrims. Today, however, droves of people make the ascent, visiting the shrines that cover the slopes of Fuji-San, the mountain of everlasting life, which dominates the horizon and captures the hearts of all that see it.

Colourful soft corals on the reefs of Sipadan Island. Almost 3000 species of fish have been recorded from this region

PARADISE ISLAND

Draw a triangle between Indonesia, the Philippines and New Guinea and you have the world's greatest hotspot of marine biodiversity. Almost 3,000 species of fish alone have been recorded from the Indo-Pacific triangle. Sipadan Island, just off the coast of Borneo, lies directly in the middle of this region. Tiny coral polyps, growing over thousands of years, have built a reef around Sipadan that is both beautiful and diverse. Theories suggest that the Indo-Pacific islands were protected from the extinctions that occurred at other coral reefs around the world during the last glaciation because the enormous number of islands and the size of the continental shelf provided a refuge for the sensitive coral organisms. Tourists now flock to the coast of Borneo to witness the result of this long history of speciation — the colour and complexity of the world's most beautiful coral reef.

A hotspot for coral reef biodiversity, the complex reef of Sipadan has been created by the growth of thousands of tiny coral polyps; it is thought that the Indo-Pacific region was a refuge for coral species during glaciations

HEART OF BORNEO

Borneo is one of the great islands of the world. It lies in the centre of the great Indo-Pacific biodiversity hotspot and, despite extensive human occupation, its rainforests are some of the best preserved on earth. The island is split into states owned by the Federation of Malaysia, Indonesia and the Sultanate of Brunei. Its political complexity is matched by a unique geology and biology, from the great watersheds of Sarawak to the remote and virtually untouched northern interior where the Segama River flows through the Danum Valley Conservation Area. This 438-kilometre square (170 square miles) region comprises one of the largest and least disturbed lowland dipterocarp – any tree of the family *Dipterocarpaceae* that has enlarged, wing-sepals to help dispurse the fruit – rainforests in the Indo-Pacific. It is home to the highly endangered Sumatran rhino, elephant, orang-utan and clouded leopard, as well as a unique and complex rainforest fauna. All eight species of the spectacular hornbill bird can be found in this single area.

The Segama River flows through lowland rainforest in Danum Valley Conservation Area. This region is one of the best preserved dipterocarp rainforests in the Indo-Pacific, and is home to the endangered Sumatran rhino

MOTHER OF THE UNIVERSE

In 1852 a young Indian mathematician named Radhanath Sikdar identified a mountain across the border of Nepal and Tibet that exceeded all others in height. Sidkar's boss, the surveyor general of India, named it after his previous boss, Sir George Everest. The word Everest now inspires and frightens — a combination irresistible to all mountaineers. At nearly 9 kilometres (29,925 feet) in height, this mountain makes nearly all others appear small; the Tibetan name for it, *Chomolangma*, means 'mother of the universe'. The first serious summit attempts were hampered by the lack of high-altitude oxygen equipment, but technological developments after the Second World War and the military planning of expedition leader John Hunt allowed climbers Edmund Hillary and Tenzing Norgay to stand on the top of Everest in 1953.

A mountaineer enjoys the view of Everest from Gokyo Ri, Khumbu, Nepal. This giant of a mountain is a lure for climbers the world over. Today it is climbed regularly from both the Nepalese and Tibetan sides

PILLARS IN THE MIST

The Wulingyuan Scenic District in China's Hunan Province is dominated by 200-metre (650 feet) high pillars of pure quartzite sandstone. Some 3,000 of these pillars rise up across the complex landscape of rivers and mountains to form one of the most spectacular geological sights in the world. A third of the district is limestone, and the underground rivers and caves present another remarkable geological story. The warm, moist climate allows plants and forests to flourish, and the region is rich in oak, maple and pine. Endangered species in the district include the Chinese giant salamander and clouded leopard, although sightings of the latter have been very rare. This beautiful region does not have a long history of human occupation; it was not until the Ming and Qing dynasties from the fourteenth century onwards that people started to use the sandstone pillars as defended villages. Although these villages are long gone, the region is now popular with tourists the world over.

The sandstone pillars of Wulingyuan Scenic District. The region is dominated by these incredible geological formations, and is home to diverse plant and animal life, including the elusive clouded leopard

Mount Kinabalu, towering above the rainforests of Borneo. The shiny granitic outcrops of the summits can be seen jutting above the rich forest, which is home to an incredible variety of species, including Rafflesia, the largest flower in the world

MOUNTAIN OF DEATH, CRADLE OF LIFE

In the native language of the Dusun people of Borneo, *Kinabalu* means 'revered place of the dead'. To scientists, Mount Kinabalu National Park is a natural wonder of geology and biology. Intrusion of lava through tertiary sedimentary rocks 1.5 million years ago has created the 4,095-metre (13,435 feet) high mountain, with its many peaks of lofty granite outcrops shining clear above the dense rainforest. The jungle itself is thought to be the richest and most diverse plant assemblage anywhere in the world. The diversity of topography, geology and past climatic oscillations has encouraged species to form – the process of speciation – in this unique national park. Between 5,000 and 6,000 species of plant have been recorded from this one park, and over 600 species of fern – more than for the whole of tropical mainland Africa. Rafflesia, the largest flower in the world, has been recorded here, as have the shy Malay bear and Borneo gibbon.

The Rock Islands of Palau.
These strange, mushroom-
shaped islands are formed
from uplifted limestone
outcrops, and have since been
so thickly covered in tropical
vegetation that they appear
to float above the water

FLOATING ISLANDS

The islands of Micronesia are one of the biodiversity hotspots of the world; the famous Rock Islands of Palau are a supreme example and are regarded as one of the seven underwater wonders of the world. These uplifted coralline limestone islands are thickly covered in tropical vegetation and appear to float above the clear blue water and reef below. Palau's proximity to the huge source of biodiversity that is Indonesia, New Guinea and the Philippines, and its variety of habitats, including mangrove forests, seagrass beds and coral reef, make it a true natural wonder. More than 420 species of hard coral and 120 species of soft coral have been recorded from the islands, as have 1,278 species of fish. Of the nine worldwide species of Tridacna, the giant clam, seven have been found in these islands alone. The islands' location at the crossroads of three major ocean currents lures major marine predators to feed close to the reefs – and over thousands of years, successive human migrations too.

The volcanic Lord Howe Island, New South Wales, showing the lagoon and Mounts Lidgbird and Gower. This beautiful island lies in a temperate latitude, yet warm waters from the north bring coral larvae and tropical species to the shallow lagoon and fringing reef

SECRET
ISLAND

Just 700 kilometres (435 miles) north-east of Sydney in an open stretch of the Pacific Ocean lies the remarkable island group of Lord Howe. Named unimaginatively for an English admiral and populated by just 350 permanent settlers, the islands are home to the world's most southerly coral reef at a latitude of 31° south; coral larvae are transported here from the more northerly Great Barrier Reef by warm ocean currents. The rugged mountains that form the main island are the tips of a 7 million-year-old extinct shield volcano that rises 4 kilometres (2.5 miles) from the ocean floor. Over 100 species of endemic plant have been recorded on the islands, and a surprising 80 species of coral live in these temperate waters. The islands, relatively undamaged by human activity, are heavily protected by the local people and authorities, with only 400 tourists allowed to stay at any one time.

WAVE ROCK

The curving, precipitous north face of Hyden Rock is one of Western Australia's best-known geological features, and yet it continues to astound all who see it. Known as Wave Rock, the 110-metre (360 feet) long granite cliff face is shaped like an enormous wave, 15 metres (50 feet) high, that looks ready to break overhead. This incredible formation, which feels like a moment frozen in time and instils an aura of pent-up power and anticipation, is actually the result of millions of years of geological evolution. However, controversy still surrounds the age and formation of Wave Rock, with estimates ranging from less than 500 million years to 3,000 million years old. Whatever the true age, the spectacular overhang appears to have resulted from erosion that first occurred under the ancient soil layer, subsequently being exposed to further weathering. The rock face is streaked with vertical bands of algae, a fitting fascia for a rock that seems imbued with the energy of life.

WALL OF LIFE

The Great Barrier Reef off the coast of Queensland in Australia comprises the largest collection of coral reefs in the world. Over 3,400 individual reefs stretch from the shores of Australia across the ocean for over 2,000 kilometres (1,245 miles) to Papua New Guinea – the world's most extensive reef system. The reefs have formed over millions of years from the limestone secretion of coral polyps – tiny colonial animals. The pounding Pacific surf and hole-boring organisms have created a complex three-dimensional marine environment. The reef is home to 400 species of living coral, 1,500 species of fish and an incredible 4,000 species of mollusc. Rare mammals such as the dugong feed there, and the reef provides nesting grounds for the endangered green and loggerhead turtles. The Great Barrier Reef and other Indo-Pacific reefs are famous for the way in which the coral polyps breed synchronously by spawning larvae into the water column in phase with lunar cycles.

CLOUD PIERCER

The great Southern Alps of New Zealand were formed by the massive collision and uplifting of the Pacific and Australian-Indian tectonic plates, which are still pushing this mountain range, and its highest peak Mount Cook, skyward by approximately 10 millimetres ($^2/_5$ inch) per year. Known in the local Kai Tahu dialect as *Aoraki*, meaning 'cloud piercer', this 3,754 metre (12,315 feet) peak is the mountaineering challenge of New Zealand. Named after the great English navigator James Cook and located in the Roaring Forties (the name applied by sailors to the latitudes between 40°S and 50°S, where the prevailing westerly winds are strong and steady), this mountain has severe weather and a challenging snow and ice route to the summit; it was first climbed by local New Zealanders in 1894. Surrounding it are more than 140 peaks over 2,000 metres (6,565 feet) in height and 72 glaciers that cover over 40 per cent of the 700 square kilometres (270 square miles) of Westland National Park.

Hooker Valley and the Mueller Glacier, leading up to Mount Cook, the highest peak in New Zealand. The mountain was named after the great English Navigator, James Cook, and was first climbed by New Zealanders in 1894

COLOURS OF THE DREAMTIME

Uluru, or Ayers Rock, may only be the second largest monolith in the world, but it is certainly the most iconic. Its feldspar-enriched arkosic sandstone shifts in colour as the sun hits it from different angles and heights. Sunset in particular is remarkable, when an intense and fiery red glow emanates from the great rock. Uluru is 335 metres (1,100 feet) high, 3.6 kilometres (2 miles) long and 2 kilometres (1.25 miles) wide. The red stone of Uluru and the surrounding desert is a result of the oxidization – or rusting – of the iron present in the soil. The sandstone that contains this iron is highly susceptible to water erosion, and the sides of Uluru are scoured and fluted into numberless, gently undulating ridges and steeply dipping fissures. The surface of the rock looks smooth from a distance but is actually covered with huge gullies – also the result of water erosion. Uluru has captured human imagination for millennia, from 10,000-year-old Aboriginal beliefs to the wonderment of the rest of the world that flock to it today.

MAGNETIC MOUNDS

In the far north of Australia an intriguing scientific puzzle presents itself in the form of magnetic termite mounds. Termite mounds are found on every continent, but it is only here that they produce tall, thin mounds that are aligned along a north-south axis. Two species of termite are known to produce magnetic mounds: *Amitermes laurensis* from Cape York Peninsula and *Amitermes meridionalis* from the Northern Territory. The termites feed mainly on the surrounding grasses that are harvested by worker termites at night and stored in special chambers inside the mounds. Early speculations on the reasons for the alignment were that it was a feature to prevent wind damage or an adaptation to speed up the drying process during mound construction. More recent theories have used measurements of internal temperature (and in some cases experimental movement of entire mounds) to demonstrate that the alignment is probably a heat-regulating mechanism — but a certain amount of mystery remains.

Magnetic mounds formed by termites in the Northern Territory. It is thought that the north-south alignment of the long axis of the mounds is an adaptation to regulate heat inside the colony

RELICS OF AN ANCIENT LAND

The Blue Mountains get their name from the veil of blue mist that appears to hang over the vast eucalyptus forests when viewed from the high sandstone escarpments; it is thought that volatile oils released from the trees interact with the light to create this strange aura. The Blue Mountains are one of the supreme examples of post-Gondwana evolutionary diversification. When Gondwana, the great supercontinent that existed 200–160 million years ago, began to break up, the early fauna started to diversify into the many hundred species we see today, some 90 of which occur in Blue Mountains National Park. While the existence of Gondwana has been strongly supported for many years by geological evidence, incredible biological corroboration came to light in 1994 with the discovery of Wollemia nobilis, the Wollemi pine, thought to be an extinct Gondwanan tree previously known only from fossils.

The Blue Mountains National Park, New South Wales. This land of sandstone escarpments and deep, forested valleys is famed for the permanent blue mist that hangs there — formed by the oils released into the air by abundant eucalyptus trees

LIFE IN LAYERS

When the former pirate and part-time sea captain for the British Admiralty, William Dampier, sailed into Shark Bay in 1699, he was displeased at the lack of anchorage, but perhaps more so at the abundance of sharks surrounding his ship. What he did not know was that the bay he named would become famous for another reason: now a World Heritage reserve, Shark Bay in Western Australia is home to 10,000 dugongs and the most ancient form of life on earth –

stromatolites. Estimated to have been in existence for 3.5 billion years, stromatolites are formed from blue-green algae that grows in layers, forming small limestone mounds on the seabed. To the geologists who discovered them, they appeared to be living fossils, previously known only from rocks. In Shark Bay, the high salinity of the warm, shallow waters inhibits the normal predators of these organisms, creating this natural wonder of the living and fossil world.

Stromatolites, colonies of blue-green algae growing in Hamelin Pool, Shark Bay. These mounds are thought to be one of the oldest known forms of life on the planet

STAR
WOUND

In the north of Australia an ancient ringed mountain system exists known as *Tnorala* by the indigenous people and Gosse Bluff to the westerners who first investigated it. Evidence suggests that it is the remnant of an eroded meteorite crater; 135 million years ago a meteorite struck here, devastating more than 20 square kilometres (8 square miles) of the desert and leaving behind the shattered rocks and signature geology of impacts – shocked quartz. Meteorites hit the earth many thousands of times per year, but the vast majority are small enough to be destroyed by the friction of the earth's atmosphere. In rare cases, meteorites that are larger than 10 metres (35 feet) in diameter will reach the ground or more commonly the ocean. The energy in a falling rock moving at over 12 kilometres (7 miles) per second is greater than its equivalent weight in conventional explosive, so that large impacts resemble nuclear-size blasts.

The giant meteor crater, Gosse Bluff, Central Desert, Australia. Known as *Tnorala* by the indigenous people, this circular mountain range is thought to be 135 million years old

LAND OF THE CROCODILE

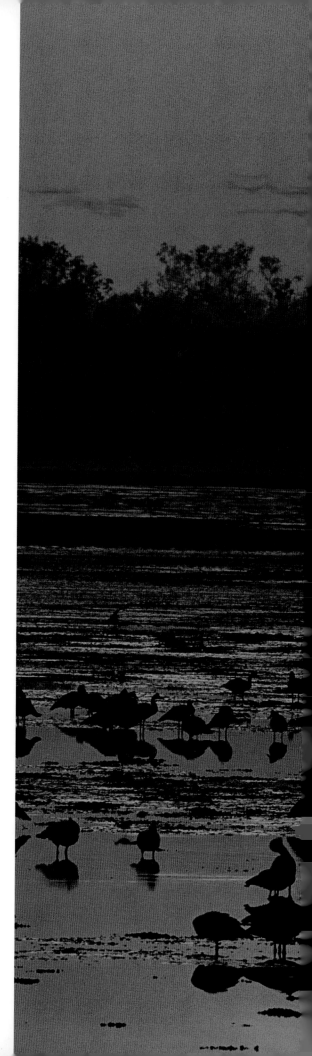

In 1818–20 the explorer Captain Phillip Parker King discovered three great rivers flowing through northern Australia into the Van Diemen Gulf, the inlet of the Timor Sea. The lower reaches were infested with what he thought were alligators, and he named these rivers somewhat unimaginatively as East, West and South Alligator River. In fact the 'alligators' were fresh- and saltwater crocodiles inhabiting the wetlands and estuaries of what is now known as Kakadu National Park. This region, inhabited for perhaps more than 50,000 years by indigenous people, is a land of extraordinary geological and biological diversity, and is home to a third of all Australian bird species and its most frightening reptiles. Local people recognize six different seasons, the most popular time to visit being post-monsoon.

Magpie Geese at sunset in Kakadu National Park. This remote and spectacular national park is home to a third of all Australian bird species, and its most dangerous reptiles, the fresh and saltwater crocodiles

LAST PLACE ON EARTH

Heard Island has a reasonable claim to being the last place on earth; it is almost certain that no human ever visited the island until Peter Kemp, a British sealer, sailed past in 1833 and recorded a sighting of the island in his log. Captain John Heard, an American sealer, later charted and officially reported the discovery, having the island named after him. Heard Island is unique among the sub-Antarctic islands – its isolation (4,100 kilometres, or 2,550 miles, from the nearest human settlement in Perth, Australia) has left it pristine, unlike the Kerguelen Islands 440 kilometres (275 miles) to the north, which are infested with introduced cats and goats. Its highest point, Big Ben, rises to 2,745 metres (9,005 feet) and is permanently covered by giant glaciers, and it is the only sub-Antarctic island with an active volcano – Mount Mawson. Sporadic scientific parties have stopped here, climbed to the summit of Big Ben and set up simple bases at Atlas Cove. Continuous weather observations on the island are used to monitor the earth's changing climate.

Heard and McDonald Islands lie in one of the remotest places on Earth — the Southern Ocean. This sub-Antarctic realm is one of volcanic islands and giant glaciers

DESERT TOMBSTONES

Created over eons but only exposed in recent centuries, the Pinnacles Desert in Australia's Nambung National Park is a geological wonder found amid beaches, coastal dunes, heath land and forested groves. Thousands of limestone pillars, some 3.5 metres (10 feet) tall, rise out of the desert sands, stretching as far as the eye can see. Likened to the crumbling remains of an ancient city or row upon row of giant tombstones, the pinnacles inspire melancholy contemplation. They grew from the ancient dune systems that line the Nambung coast; the dunes' lime-rich sands dissolved in the rainfalls of the winter months and then solidified to form tamala limestone. A thick bed of this limestone once covered the region, but over thousands of years it was eroded by rain, wind and the action of plant growth, leaving behind spectacular monoliths. The continually shifting desert sands, blown by southerly winds, mean the pinnacles are only transiently visible, with the southern pillars being slowly and relentlessly engulfed by the sands of this dynamic natural environment.

The great rock pinnacles of Nambung National Park, Western Australia. The rocks are formed from ancient limestones, dissolved by rainfall and subsequently surrounded by sand

SUPERVOLCANIC
LAKES

Hidden beneath the large lakes of the North Island of New Zealand is an explosive historical past. Volcanologists have devised a scale of explosivity for large volcanoes, both those in the historical record and those that have happened in geological time. According to geological records, Lake Taupo has erupted 28 times in the last 27,000 years and the most recent eruption, in AD 181, is thought to have ejected a plume of ash over 50 kilometres (30 miles) high, twice as high as the plume ejected from Mount St Helens in North America in 1980. This puts Lake Taupo at the point of mega-colossal events on the volcanic explosivity index. The area seems calm now, but the continued geothermal energy is still visible in the bubbling pools of mud of the Rotorua area.

Boiling mudpots in the Rotorua area, North Island, New Zealand. This region is heavily influenced by both past and present volcanism. The geothermal pools of Rotorua are a tiny relic of the giant volcanic calderas that once formed here

An aerial view of the Osmond Range, Bungle Bungle Range. The dome-shaped towers of the Bungle Bungles rise above the desert plains, and are an example of cone 'karst' formations, rich in iron and manganese

BUNGLE BUNGLE

The Bungle Bungle Range in Purnululu National Park in Western Australia is a superlative example of a geological wonder. From a desert plain, great dome-shaped towers rise up 300 metres (985 feet). These are the relics of mountains created some 300 million years ago, and have been dissolving over the last 20 million years. They are the supreme example of cone karst formations, a phenomenon not fully understood by scientists. Bungle Bungle's sandstone pillars are coloured by alternating stripes of orange and grey. This strange effect is caused by some rock layers letting in more water than others and being colonized by a type of algae. The drier layers oxidize at the edges to produce an orange crust. Made of iron- and manganese-rich sandstone, they are an outstanding example of the way in which geology and biology can interact to create dramatic landscapes.

FOREST MOSAIC

In north-east Australia, the rainforests of Queensland and New South Wales occur as patches in a sea of fire-prone eucalyptus. Where annual rainfall exceeds 1,500 millimetres (60 inches), usually in the upland regions, lush forests fill the gullies and sometimes the larger valleys of the area. These patches are the living remnants of the great forests that covered the ancient Gondwanan supercontinent that included Australia, Antarctica, Africa, India and South America. During the break-up of Gondwana 150–100 million years ago, the first flowering plants evolved, and scientists today can trace this evolutionary radiation to these unique forests. Tourists to the region can visit these habitats and view the spectacular geology that includes giant calderas and escarpments formed by 20 million-year-old volcanic ranges. The rainforest also supports Australia's largest numbers of frog, snake, bird and marsupial species.

Millamilla Falls in the Atherton Tablelands. This unique region is a supreme example of Gondwanan vegetation — the lush forests that once covered the great continent 150 million years ago. Only small areas of the original rainforest exist

EUROPE

Europe is the second smallest continent after Australasia, but is the region of the world where the modern understanding and exploration of the globe began. As a consequence of Europe's political importance in historical times, many natural wonders are seen from a distinctly Eurocentric viewpoint – early explorers considered the wonders of distant lands to be incredible and exotic in comparison to those of their European homelands. This masks the diversity and complexity of Europe's own natural beauty spots and, while the long period of high population density has meant that the isolation and vast, open wildernesses found elsewhere in the world disappeared long ago, many natural wonders can still be found here.

Forming a fifth of the Eurasian landmass, the boundaries of Europe (and hence Asia) are politically defined on its eastern borders. The continent ranges from the Arctic in the north to the islands of the Mediterranean Sea in the south, and climate changes across its latitudinal gradient. From the northerly tundra, it ranges southwards through taiga, deciduous forests, steppe and the distinctive, aromatic Mediterranean maquis flora. Where forest remains untouched by humans, a glimpse of a past Europe can be caught, where wild beasts roamed and trees covered the land.

So much of Europe has been shaped by its very long history. The ancient rocks of the mountains have been scoured into deep valleys, and eroded over the eons so that they do not rival the height of their younger Asian neighbours. The last Ice Age, when much of the northern region was engulfed by huge ice sheets, left dramatic fjords and valleys across the continent. It also left its mark on fauna and animal life, with many of Europe's ancient fauna and creatures such as the mammoth, giant elk and big cats disappearing with the ice.

Europe's geological past is more apparent than its biological one, mostly due to human activity, and the mountains, rivers and volcanic formations are as spectacular as elsewhere in the world. Indeed, the unexpectedness of natural beauty among arable and urban landscapes creates its own wonder – nature's ability to survive the ravages of humankind.

GLACIAL VALLEYS

During the great Ice Ages of the Quaternary period, 2 million years ago, enormous glaciers carved out the river channels of Norway's west coast, creating the relief that would later form the famous U-shaped valleys of the fjords. They are found the world over, but in Norway they are most spectacular; the rise in sea levels following the retreat of the great ice sheets at the end of the Pleistoscene epoch created seawater-flooded valleys that can reach over 200 kilometres (125 miles) in length. The water of the fjords is cool, dark and rich in specialist marine life; in recent years marine biologists have discovered large beds of an unusual cold-water coral reef created by the organism *Lophelia pertusa*. These reef beds are home to high biodiversity and are thought to be important fish nurseries.

The Geiranger fjord is one of many beautiful fjords found in Norway. Fjords are flooded U-shaped valleys carved out by glaciers, and those in Norway are the result of the last ice age. As the ice retreated to expose these valleys, the sea levels also rose and flooded them

THE DARKEST DAY

A total eclipse of the sun is a superlative example of a natural wonder. The relationship of humans with the fiery celestial body is one of reliance, superstition and awe. From prehistory to today's scientific era, humankind has understood the importance of sunlight, relying on the regularity and predictability of the seasons for survival. Consequently, the sudden disappearance of the sun in daylight hours is an event that has instilled fear and been seen as portentous for millennia. Even today, when we understand that it is merely the predictable phenomenon of the full moon coming between the earth and the sun, so that the moon's shadow sweeps a narrow path across the face of the planet, a solar eclipse is unsettling and awe inspiring. Its wonder stems from its seeming unnaturalness and from its rareness – total eclipses happen every 18 months somewhere on earth, but the narrowness of the band of totality means that it only happens in the same place every 400 years. The last total eclipse to sweep across Europe occurred in 1999.

This multiple exposure picture shows the procession of the sun as it was eclipsed by the moon in 1991

BIRTHPLACE OF ICEBERGS

On the west coast of Greenland 250 kilometres (155 miles) inside the Arctic Circle, the Sermeq Kujalleq glacier, part of the Greenland ice cap, reaches the sea at the Ilulissat Icefjord. Every year, 35,000 cubic metres (114,359 cubic feet) of ice is 'calved' from Sermeq Kujalleq into the icy fjord, making it the most active glacier in the northern hemisphere. Ice calving is the process by which icebergs break from glaciers at their interface with the sea, and only in Antarctica does ice calving occur at a higher rate than in the Ilulissat Icefjord. The Sermeq Kujalleq glacier is one of the world's fastest moving glaciers, moving at a rate of 19 metres (60 feet) per day and producing a range of disconcerting and dramatic noises to break the silence of this remote part of the world. A remnant of the great ice that once covered much of northern Europe and America, this place of astounding beauty has an equally important role in scientific studies of climate change – past, present and future.

An iceberg floats in the Ilulissat Fjord. This iceberg is one of many that are 'calved' from the Sermeq Kujalleq Glacier, part of the Greenland ice cap, into the sea every year

FALLS OF STONE

In western Croatia an 8-kilometre (5 mile) chain of lakes and waterfalls forms the remarkable Plitvice National Park. Two mountain streams at Plitvicki Ljeskovac join to form the Matica River, which feeds Lake Prosce, the first in the series. The remarkable waterfalls, grottos and caves that are the highlights of Plitvice are formed by a unique combination of chemistry and biology. Biodynamic travertine is formed when calcium carbonate in the water flows over mosses, algae and bacteria, and can grow at rates of up to 10 millimetres ($2/5$ inch) per year. This constantly moving platform has created over 20 lakes, and waterfalls up to 80 metres (260 feet) high. The Plitvice and Sastavci falls are most spectacular during periods of snowmelt. The 14,000 hectares (34,590 acres) of forest that surround the lakes are rich in beech and fir, and home to the European brown bear and wolf.

The waterfalls of the Plitvice Lakes, western Croatia. Over 20 lakes have been created by the moving platform of 'biodynamic travertine', as have many remarkable waterfalls

MOUNTAINS SHAPED BY ICE

In the far north of Scotland the true power of the great Quaternary's – the geological time period of the last 1.8 million years – ice sheets can be seen. Ice up to 1 kilometre (0.6 mile) thick flowed across the northern latitudes of Europe 18,000 years ago, creating valleys and eroding ancient mountains into the spectacular land forms we see today, such as Suilven in Scotland, thought to be the most beautiful mountain in the Highlands. Derived from Norse and meaning 'Pillar Mountain', this isolated monolith is located deep in the Sutherland moors; despite appearing unclimbable, it is easily reached by a scrambling route along the main summit ridge. Over 100 lochs (lakes) and lochans (small lakes) are visible from the summit – an implausibly broad grassy plateau and the best point from which to survey one of Europe's last great wilderness regions.

The whole of Scotland and most of England were covered by ice, some 18,000 years ago. When the ice retreated it left behind the incredible highland scenery of today, from the slopes of the beautiful Suilven, pictured here in the distance, to the myriad lochs of the region

DEEP BLUE CHASM

The word lake does not do justice to the mighty rift that splits southern Siberia. Nearly 2,000 metres (6,565 feet) of water and another 7,000 metres (22,965 feet) of sediment hide a trench that rivals anything in the ocean for depth. Lake Baikal is the world's deepest lake and has the largest volume of water – 20 per cent of all the fresh water on the planet. Formed some 25 million years ago, the lake has developed its own unique and diverse range of species, including the unusual Baikal seal. Theories suggest that the seal reached the lake via a previous opening into the Arctic Sea, but it appears miraculous. To Russians the lake is their Grand Canyon, but its scientific importance far exceeds that. The sediments in the bottom remain untouched by glacial activity and provide a unique record of climate change over the past 250,000 years. Current technology has limited the sampling of these sediments, but in the future scientists will take much deeper cores that will go back millions of years in time.

Lake Baikal is the world's deepest lake, containing a staggering 20 per cent of all the fresh water on earth. The lake was formed 25 million years ago, and is home to unique species, including the Baikal seal

ICE MAIDEN

The Bernese Oberland in Switzerland is the longest continuous mountain range in the Alps. Its 100 kilometres of lofty peaks, including those icons of early alpinism, the Eiger and the breathtakingly beautiful Jungfrau, rise to the north of the Rhône. The region was formed 20–30 million years ago, but was further sculpted by the glaciers of the last Ice Age to produce spectacular U-shaped valleys, moraine – earth, rock and stone accumulated through glacial action – crevasses and glacial lakes. It still remains the most glaciated region in the Alps, with Europe's largest and longest glacier, the Aletsch, being found there. The Aletsch is 24 kilometres (15 miles) long and covers 171 square kilometres (70 square miles) of mountain terrain. In places the ice is 900 metres (2,955 feet) thick, and its glacial tongues descend lower into the valleys than any other European glacier. While the highest peak is the Finsteraarhorn at 4,724 metres (15, 500 feet), it is the undeniably glacial beauty of the Jungfrau that dominates this rugged mountain ridge.

Three great mountains of the Bernese Oberland. From right to left, the Eiger, Monch and the beautiful Jungfrau. The region was formed over 20 million years ago, and sculpted by glaciers to produce today's spectacular scenery

THE GREAT GEYSIR

Iceland is a region of high geothermal activity, contrasting spectacularly with its glaciated landscape. The many hot springs and fumeroles of the island are famous throughout the world, and Iceland's economy relies heavily on the geothermal energy derived from them. *Geysir* is an Icelandic word meaning 'to rush forth'. After large earthquakes in the thirteenth century shook the south-west of Iceland, initiating large eruptions of boiling water from hot springs in the region of Árnes, the term was used to name the Great Geysir. After fame of its turbulent and impressive eruptions spread, its name became synonymous with similar phenomena worldwide. Since its first documented eruption in 1294, its activity has declined, no longer reaching the famed heights of 60 metres (195 feet). It is still a formidable sight, however – the water of the Great Geysir reaches a temperature of 240°C (464°F) below ground and erupts daily from its 18-metre (60 feet) wide pool.

The Icelandic word geysir means 'to rush forth'; expressive of the violent expulsion of superheated water from beneath the earth. Iceland's region of Geysir has lent its name to this geothermal phenomenon

MAGICAL CARPET

Amid woody groves and forests, where dappled light breaks through the newly green canopies, the British bluebell, *Hyacinthoides nonscripta*, blooms. The purple-blue, bell-shaped flowers hang from their arching stems and sway in the spring breezes. The delicate beauty of a solitary bluebell, though uncontested, is incomparable with the spectacle of a bluebell wood. These flowering plants are able to grow in such close proximity that they can form unbroken expanses of dusky blue, carpeting the woodland floor in a profusion of flowers to herald the season of new growth. Growing and flowering before the leaves of the trees block out the sunlight, the bluebell dominates the undergrowth, creating a magical atmosphere. However, this domination of the woodland masks vulnerability. *Hyacinthoides nonscripta* is disappearing, and being replaced by the Spanish bluebell and its hybrids. Without careful protection, the wildflower that has defined British springtime for centuries may be lost for good.

This bluebell wood is swathed in the purple haze that is so characteristic of the British springtime

PENINSULA OF FIRE

In the north-west corner of the Pacific Ocean, one of the finest examples of oceanic plate subduction can be found. This is the region where the Pacific plate is being forced slowly north-west by the action of powerful movement in the molten magma deep inside the earth. Moving at a rate of approximately 80 millimetres (3 inches) per year, the plate is being forced slowly under the Kamchatka Peninsula, and the associated volcanism has created a chain of large, explosive stratovolcanoes, such as Karimsky, one of the most active. The result of this small yet continual movement is that most of the volcanic cones of Kamchatka have been formed only within the last 20,000 years, making it incredibly young in geological terms. For the native people of Kamchatka, the land is never quiet, yet this region is one of unique beauty and abundant natural resources.

The Avachinskij volcano is one of the chain of explosive stratovolcanoes of the Kamchatka peninsula. The volcanism of this region is the result of the Pacific plate being forced under the peninsula, one of the finest examples of oceanic plate subduction in the world

BRIDGE OF MYTH

The Giant's Causeway on the north-east coast of Northern Ireland is steeped in centuries of folklore. Unsurprisingly, the bizarre, basaltic rock formations have inspired storyteller and scientist alike to search for the origins of this remarkable region of outstanding natural beauty. The causeway's mythical genesis is attributed to the giant Finn MacCumhaill, who is said to have constructed the causeway to reach the Hebridean isle of Staffa, the home of his true love. Its real origins are no less exciting – born out of volcanic eruptions some 60 million years ago, the successive cooling of lava produced the 40,000 hexagonal columns of basalt we see today. These tightly packed, interlocking pillars, some of which reach 25 metres (80 feet) in height, stretch for 6 kilometres (4 miles) along the coast, making up the largest remaining lava plateau in Europe. The Giant's Causeway, which descends from the cliffs to disappear beneath the crashing waves, is one of those rare places where fairytale and science can flourish side by side.

The Giant's Causeway, is said to be the work of a mythical giant. Science, however, attributes this fantastical formation to volcanic eruptions that left behind 40,000 hexagonal basaltic columns

GLACIAL MOUNTAIN

Mont Blanc is the highest of all Alpine peaks at 4,807 metres (15,770 feet). The massif is permanently covered by 100 square kilometres (40 square miles) of glaciers, giving rise to its name, which means 'white mountain', and straddles the borders of France, Italy and Switzerland. A glacier engulfs the summit of Mont Blanc, creating a dome of ice that smoothes the mountain's rugged profile and that varies in thickness from year to year. Changing climatic conditions can cause as much as a 3-metre (10 feet) fluctuation in glacier thickness, thereby affecting the height of the summit. Mont Blanc's glaciers, which descend the slopes from the summit to within 800 metres (2,625 feet) of local towns, ensure that this is one of the most dynamic and ever changing peaks in the Alps. The Mer de Glace, meaning sea of ice, is a 200-metre (655 feet) deep glacier that extends for 560 metres (1,835 feet), making it the second longest glacier in the Alps. The glaciers grow and retreat in response to the climate; in the seventeenth century they engulfed the Chamonix Valley, destroying farmland and homesteads.

The highest of all alpine peaks, Mont Blanc straddles the borders between France, Italy and Switzerland. Its slopes and peaks, including the summit, are permanently covered by glaciers which affect the actual height of the mountain from season to season, depending on climatic fluctuation

The Danube delta is home to 50 per cent of the world's breeding population of white pelicans

DANUBE RIVER

The Danube Delta covers 4,300 square kilometres (1,660 square miles), only 9 per cent of which is permanently above water, and is the largest continuous marshland in Europe. Made up of three main river channels connected via numerous freshwater lakes that empty into the Black Sea amid vast expanses of aquatic vegetation, the delta is thought to have formed relatively recently. The ancient River Danube emptied into the Black Sea in a shallow cove that began to fill with silt towards the very end of the last Ice Age. Every year the river deposits alluvial silt into the delta, extending it seawards by 30 metres (100 feet) annually and continually reshaping the sandbars and riverbanks of this complex environment. The flooded reed beds, riverine forests and floating islands support an impressive array of bird life, notably half the world's breeding population of white pelicans and 95 per cent of the world's wintering population of red-breasted goose. The delta is also home to rare sturgeons – ancient freshwater fish that grow to over 7 metres (25 feet) in length.

The Danube river meanders past the thickly forested banks of the Wachau Valley in Austria. The ruins of Durnstein Castle are in the foreground

DISTANT ISLES

The St Kilda island group is the most remote of all inhabited places in the British Isles. The four islands — Hirta, Soay, Boreray and Dun — are situated 64 kilometres (40 miles) west of the Outer Hebrides in the North Atlantic Ocean. The remains of a ring volcano scoured by the glaciers of the last Ice Age, the islands' spectacular sea cliffs are a refuge for rare sea birds. The vertical sea stacks and cliffs of Boreray house the world's largest gannet colony, and the St Kilda archipelago also contains Britain's largest and oldest fulmar colony as well as 50 per cent of Britain's puffin population. The precipitous cliffs of St Kilda tower out of the turbulent waters; the north face of Conachair Hill reaches 430 metres (1,410 feet), making it the highest sea cliff in Europe. Humans have lived here for thousands of years, despite the isolation. However, the last permanent population was evacuated to the mainland in the 1930s, leaving the islands to a handful of transient workers and a vast number of sea birds.

The islands of St Kilda are the most remote of all inhabited parts of the British Isles. They have the highest sea cliffs in Europe, and are a refuge for sea birds like the puffin

THE BADLANDS OF THE MOON

Deep in the north-east Atlantic a hotspot in the earth's crust has created one of the great volcanic island chains of the world, the Canary Islands. First mentioned by the Roman writer Pliny in AD 40 and inhabited by humans for thousands of years since, these islands were the great explorers' staging post on the way to the New World; Columbus himself replenished all four of his westbound fleets here. Lanzarote is one of the oldest of the islands, yet the low rainfall – only 115 millimetres (5 inches) per year – has prevented extensive plant cover, and the volcanic relics of this island are very visible. Unusual endemic plant species are found here, and the beaches are often marked by stretches of black sand – formed from the rapid cooling of lava. Lanzarote also has unique anchialine cave habitats – isolated marine habitats, landlocked for thousands of years and home to unique, ancient lineages of animals.

An aerial view of the Montanas del Fuego, Lanzarote. The black sand of the beaches of Lanzarote, and the spectacularly bleak chains of extinct volcanoes, has created a landscape likened to the surface of the moon

The Bialowieza Forest bison, the last species of wild bison left on the continent. Other rare animals — vestiges of Europe's wild past — to have made their home in this remarkable woodland include the grey wolf, beaver, lynx, elk and wild boar

WILD WOOD

In the north-east of Poland, crossing the border into Belarus, the last vestiges of Europe's primeval forests cast a dark and esoteric shadow, hinting at the wild heart of today's sophisticated continent. Within this Palaearctic realm, where the Norwegian spruce reaches its southern limit and the cessile oak reaches its northern extent, a unique fauna roams — relics of ancient Europe. European bison, grey wolf, beaver, lynx, otter, elk, red deer, roe deer and wild boar also remain here, as do cranes, storks and many raptors — a combination of beasts that seemed banished to the history books, or the tangle-wood of fairytales. Made up of Poland's Bialowieza Forest and the Belovezhaskaya Pushcha National Park of Belarus, this contiguous stretch of woodland covers a combined area of over 980 square kilometres (375 square miles), a tiny fragment of a habitat that once covered great swathes of the continent.

A shady forest pool deep within the Bialowieza Forest. The last remnant of the great, primeval forests that once covered much of Europe

The dramatic scenery of
Corsica is created by the
ancient inland granite
mountain ranges that
are set amidst classic
Mediterranean maquis flora

THE SCENTED ISLE

Corsica's scenery is among the most dramatic in Europe. With an area of 8,680 square kilometres (3,350 square miles), two-thirds of this Mediterranean island is mountainous and the rest is characterized by sheer cliffs. Splitting the island along its north-west to south-west axis is an ancient mountain range made from a crystalline, granite massif that shows distinctive porphyritic rock features. Porphyritic rocks contain crystals that indicate a complex volcanic origin and, in Corsica, can be vividly coloured. The irregular structure of the rocks creates the distinctive jagged silhouettes of the Corsican mountains for which they are renowned. The toughest of all Europe's *Grandes Randoneés* hiking routes, GR20, crosses this beautiful mountain range, the highest point being Mount Cinto at 2,710 metres (8,890 feet). The vegetation on Corsica is a supreme example of the classic Mediterranean maquis flora, which is made up of aromatic, evergreen shrubs such as cork oak, laurel and myrtle whose fragrance carries far out to sea, giving Corsica its other name – the Scented Isle.

VIRGIN FORESTS

The Komi forests of the northern Ural Mountains in Russia are Europe's largest expanse of virgin boreal forest, and the only place in Europe where the Siberian pine grows. This land of taiga, tundra and glaciated massifs, covering 32,800 square kilometres (12,665 square miles), is a sub-polar region of unparalleled beauty and biodiversity – sphagnum bogs rife with cranberries, bilberries and cloudberries; groves of rowan and willow; vast expanses of boreal forests, with pines, firs, larches and spruces reaching up to the foothills of the Urals. The dramatic mountains and karst formations are home to rare and beautiful animals; brown bear still roam here, as do elk, reindeer, grey wolf, wolverine, sable, mink, lynx and otter, and the rivers of Komi play host to the magnificent spawning of salmon year after year. The Komi forests are Europe's best hope for preserving its endangered taiga ecosystem and retaining its beauty for years to come.

The virgin Komi forests. These are the largest expanses of boreal forest in Europe, rich in firs, larches, pines, brown bears and glaciated massifs

ISLANDS
OF THE GODS

To the ancient Greeks they were home to Aeolus, god of the winds. To the Romans they were the furnace of Vulcan, blacksmith to the gods and god of the underworld. Today they are simply the Aeolian Islands, a chain of islands to the north of Sicily that are the summits of volcanoes partially submerged beneath the Tyrrhenian Sea. Their fiery origins are still very much in evidence. The island of Stromboli remains the most active volcano on earth, having erupted several times an hour for at least the last 2,000 years; the island of Vulcan gave its name to volcanoes the world over. The islands rise to around 900 metres (2,955 feet) above sea level, their bases hidden under the waves. Humans have lived on the islands for 7,000 years, in the shadow of these unpredictable and explosive giants, and people still come from all over the world to witness the incandescent beauty of Stromboli, the lighthouse of the Mediterranean.

The volcanic island of Stromboli erupts. Humans have lived next to the volcanoes of the Aeolian islands for thousands of years, inspiring both legends of the underworld and geological research alike

PYRAMID OF THE ALPS

The Matterhorn rises pyramid-like above the Swiss town of Zermatt, dominating the horizon. Its 4,478-metre (14,695 feet) summit appears isolated, ringed by glaciers at its base, but the Matterhorn is actually the end of a mountain ridge that continues across the border into Italy. The result of many glaciers gouging out steep valleys that eventually joined up, leaving behind a sheer-faced, horn-shaped peak, the Matterhorn is a picture-perfect mountain. Its steep slopes, easily discernible as north, south, east and west faces, and sheer ridges put off Alpine mountaineers for many years, making the Matterhorn the last major Alpine summit to be conquered. Edward Whymper, Peter Taugwalder Sr and Peter Taugwalder Jr, the only three surviving members of an ill-fated group, eventually climbed the Matterhorn in 1865. Charles Hudson, Francis Douglas, Michel Croz and Douglas Hadow perished during the ascent after Hadow slipped and dragged the others to their death.

THE POLES

The Poles of the earth form our last remaining wilderness regions; to the casual observer they seem virtually untouched by human hand.

The Arctic and the Antarctic have similarities and differences. The Arctic is an ocean, with the North Pole a geographical dot in the middle of it. The Antarctic is a giant continent, almost twice the size of Australia, and the South Pole lies atop the 3,000-metre (9,845 feet) high ice sheet, a 30 million-year-old pile of snow that has never melted. Both are lands of ice, either floating on the sea, as in the Arctic, or locked in the giant continental ice sheet that is the Antarctic.

Ice is a remarkable and unusual property of water – rock solid to the touch, yet actually less dense than liquid water. This allows it to float, either as sea ice a few metres thick, or as a 300-metre (2,625 feet) high giant iceberg. To humans, the wondrous variety of forms that the ice takes in these regions inspires wonder and awe, and it is in the Poles that we find some of the most spectacular shapes and scenery in the natural world.

Although both regions are cold, the Antarctic is the coldest. The continent is isolated from the warm waters of the Indian, Pacific and Atlantic oceans by a unique and vital feature – the circumpolar current. This traps the cold Antarctic sea, and it was the development of this current that first turned Antarctica from the warm, forested continent it once was into the icy realm we know today, perhaps 30 million years ago.

In the Arctic, the sea ice comes and goes with the fluctuating climate of the planet. At the moment the earth is warming up as the result of human activities, and the Arctic ocean is losing its sea ice as the sea temperature rises and the ice melts away. In the Antarctic, many of the glaciers of the Peninsula region are retreating, and in recent years we have witnessed the first ice sheets starting to break up. Scientists think the Poles are the first regions on earth to have their geography significantly altered by global warming, a prelude to what may happen to the rest of the planet.

MOUNT EREBUS

Situated on Ross Island, Erebus is the most active volcano in Antarctica, and the most southerly explosive stratovolcano in the world. Sir James Clark Ross, the British polar explorer, discovered the mountain in 1841 and named it after his ship HMS *Erebus*. The volcano contains one of only three active lava lakes in the world, and the glow of the lava in the summit cone has been seen from space. The upper slopes of Erebus are dominated by great lava flows and lava bombs, the relics of previous eruptions. The lava lake itself periodically explodes and flows out from the summit caldera. The 3,794-metre (12,445 feet) high Mount Erebus lies close to McMurdo Station, the largest scientific base on the Antarctic continent, and its eruptions are a constant reminder of the geology of this vast, icy land. Many of the great polar explorers of the twentieth century visited Ross Island and made camps there; remarkably the mountain was first climbed in 1908.

The ice-capped volcano, Mount Erebus. The crater on the summit of this active volcano contains a lava lake, one of only three in the world. The summit of Erebus is visible from the large scientific bases at McMurdo Sound

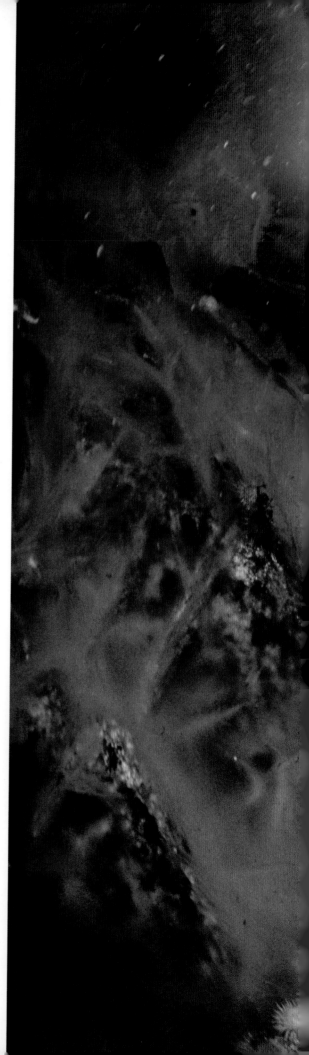

Frozen underwater waterfalls, Victoria Land. Where fresh water from melting snow trickles down a rock face, it freezes on contact with the sea water, creating remarkable formations. Marine biologists have observed abundant life beneath these ice sheets

UNDERWATER FALLS

During winter in Antarctica the ocean surrounding the continent freezes solid to a depth of 1 metre (3 feet) or more, yet this does not deter marine biologists who routinely dive beneath the ice. Remarkable formations can be seen, and the nutrient-poor waters are some of the clearest in the world. At a place called Couloir Cliffs in Victoria Land, fresh water from melting snow trickles down a rock face and seeps out beneath the sea ice layer, freezing on contact with the sea water. This creates the bizarre phenomenon of underwater waterfalls of ice apparently flowing down a submerged rock face. The sea water itself often starts to freeze onto the sea-floor boulders, creating what is called anchor ice. Despite this, abundant marine life is found, including the sea urchin *Sterechinus neumayeri*, a predatory animal that moves along the bottom searching for organisms that have become trapped in anchor ice.

EMPERORS OF THE ICE

Winter on the Antarctic ice shelf is extreme. The temperature plummets to less than -50°C (-58°F), and blizzards and high winds take possession of this frozen continent. The emperor penguin is, perhaps, the only creature not to abhor this hostile environment. It is the largest of the penguin species, with males reaching 1.1 metres (3.5 feet) tall. The male incubates its eggs over the long winter months, not feeding, but just resting the egg on its feet and warming it within his abdominal pouch. The male penguins huddle together for warmth when incubating, and yet their body temperature drops so low that snow settles on them. Emperor penguin colonies are inland, so after laying the egg the female has to walk up to 160 kilometres (100 miles) to hunt fish, squid and krill in the Southern Ocean, in elegant dives akin to underwater flight. She returns to feed and nurture the chick through the remaining winter months after it hatches, relieving the male of his onerous duty.

An emperor penguin colony in the shadow of an ice cliff. Late in the breeding season, this colony is a mixture of adults and grey four-month old chicks

DEEP BLUE ICE

In the coldest place on earth the largest glaciers of the world are found. Antarctica is so cold that snow never melts, and over millions of years it has formed an ice sheet 2.5 kilometres (1.5 miles) thick that covers the entire continent. The older the ice, the more compressed it is, and the deeper the blue that is reflected when sunlight does finally reach it. When the Antarctic ice sheet reaches the Trans-Antarctic Mountains, the great glaciers are formed, among them the Beardmore glacier, the largest in the world at over 160 kilometres (100 miles) long. When a glacier flows over terrain, stresses in the ice create the faults and movement that open up crevasses, forming treacherous obstacles to climbers. These temporary, inhospitable places are barren of life, yet lure explorers who seek the raw beauty of a land form made from something as simple as frozen water.

A climber negotiates a crevasse on the Antarctic Peninsula. The great ice sheet that covers Antarctica represents millions of years of snow fall. Where the great glaciers of Antarctica move through mountainous regions, crevasses such as this one are formed

LIFE BENEATH THE ICE

In Antarctica, the frozen continent, the greatest diversity and abundance of life is beneath the waves and quite often beneath the ice. Winter temperatures are so cold that sea water freezes and a layer of ice up to 20 million square kilometres (7,722,045 square miles) in extent surrounds the entire continent. In the Ross Sea, adventurous marine biologists routinely melt holes in the sea ice to investigate and experiment in the shallow marine realm. For these lucky few, it is an astounding experience; the lack of sunlight and nutrients during the winter months keeps the water clear, and divers can see for hundreds of metres around them. On the sea floor, abundant marine life in the form of sponges, anemones, worms and molluscs await the summer bloom of life, when food and nutrients return to these clear waters.

A diver hovers beneath thick sea ice in the Antarctic. Low sunlight and nutrient levels during the winter keep the water clear from plankton, creating stunning visibility in the water. Abundant marine life carpets the ocean floor, awaiting the return of summer, and nutrients to fuel the ocean ecosystem

SHEET OF ICE

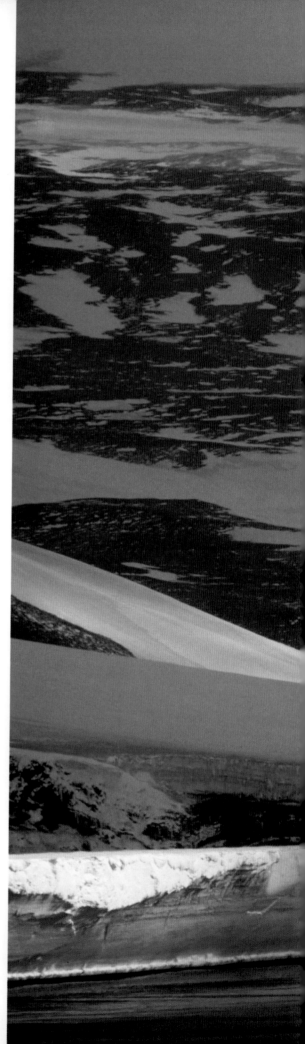

On the continent of Antarctica, the temperatures are so low that snow never melts. Over thousands of years, the constant build-up of snow and ice has created the giant west and east Antarctic ice sheets, which themselves feed glaciers and ice streams that flow out towards the coast. Where these ice streams reach the sea, they form giant floating ice shelves, seemingly permanently attached to the land. The Ross ice shelf is the largest of these, and is approximately the size of France. Where it ends, a floating barrier of ice 60 metres (200 feet) high is formed. The Ross ice shelf was the site of early Antarctic exploration; Roald Amundsen landed his team there, and travelled by dog sled to the Pole in 1911. Scientists have measured the thickness of the ice and sampled the ocean life beneath by drilling through it. Ice shelves such as those in the Ross Sea have in recent years started to release giant tabular icebergs into the ocean, which is disturbingly thought to indicate the initial stages of global warming in the Antarctic region.

COLD COAST

In the late sixteenth century, while searching for the Northeast Passage, the Dutch navigator and explorer Willem Barents discovered the archipelago of Svalbard – now sometimes known as Spitsbergen – in the high Arctic Ocean. The name *Svalbard* means 'cold coast', and over 60 per cent of the land is covered by permanent glaciers and snowfields. The islands are so far north that from mid-April to mid-August the sun never sets, and from mid-October to mid-February the islands are in perpetual darkness. Despite the harsh temperatures, life flourishes here although plants are limited to shrubs, lichens and mosses. It is the breeding ground of the barnacle goose, and is home to four mammal species: the Svalbard field mouse, the Arctic fox, the Svalbard reindeer and the polar bear. The bears outnumber humans, and precautions are necessary for anyone who ventures out of populated areas, although the animals are a protected species.

ICY DANCE
OF THE SOLAR WIND

Where the earth is coldest and its magnetic field strongest, aurora will illuminate the night sky. Solar wind from space bombards the earth's magnetic field, flooding it with charged subatomic particles that move towards the North and South Poles. In the upper atmosphere, these particles collide with oxygen and nitrogen gas to produce a ring of light that dances around the Poles. From earth we see an ever shifting glow of green and red, a source of wonder and speculation over the centuries. Current generations are the first to witness the full beauty of the aurora, with photographs that reveal myriad changing colours that were previously invisible to the naked eye.

An aurora borealis lights up the night sky. Auroras are formed when solar wind reaches the earth's magnetic field, bombarding nitrogen and oxygen gas molecules to produce light. The magnetic field concentrates these particles in the polar regions, where the aurora is most spectacular

ICE ISLAND

Greenland, the largest island of ice and snow in the world, was named by Scandinavian settlers determined to encourage others to follow in their footsteps. The name may not be apt, but Inuit people have lived here for centuries, with occasional gaps during periods of glacial cooling. Greenland has the second largest ice cap in the world after Antarctica, and holds 10 per cent of the ice on the planet. The great mountains of the Watkins Range extend along the east coast; partly buried by the ice sheet, the granite spires are known as *nunataks*, and are a formidable climbing challenge. The highest peak is Gunnbjorn at 3,700 metres (12,140 feet); many other unclimbed peaks lie close by, and regular expeditions attempt them. The ice sheet of Greenland is almost 3,000 metres (9,845 feet) thick in places, and scientists have drilled ice cores that provide a record of the past 100,000 years of climate change on earth.

The thick ice sheet that covers Greenland buries most mountains, except for the spires of 'nunataks' — mountains poking out through the ice. These steep-sided peaks are a great climbing challenge

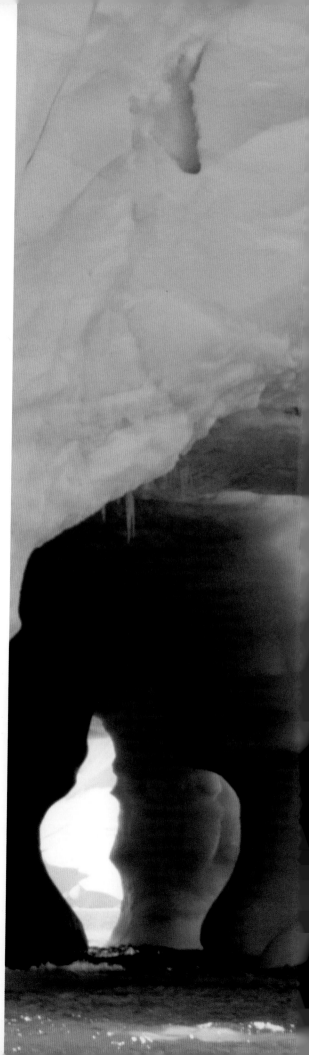

This iceberg in the Southern Ocean, has begun to melt — the action of water and waves has created a tunnel, perhaps by exploiting an old crevasse. Ninety percent of an iceberg actually lies below the ocean surface and like ships, they frequently run aground

ICEBERG

Water is remarkable in all its forms; as solid ice it can be both beautiful and dangerous – an iceberg can create the same fear and fascination as volcanoes, mountains or wild animals. One of water's unique properties is its lower density when frozen, and this allows the solid ice of glaciers and ice sheets to float when it reaches the ocean. The continual movement of ice across the Antarctic continent, coupled with the stress of tidal action on ice shelves, has created some of the largest icebergs in history, including the famous berg B15 that had an area of 11,000 square kilometres (4,245 square miles) when it broke off the Ross ice shelf in 2000. Although icebergs float, around 90 per cent of their volume is under water, and they frequently run aground in coastal regions, scouring the sea floor and sometimes causing a shipping hazard.

TAIN OF ICE

The highest mountain in Antarctica was unknown until 1957, when it was spotted by a US Navy reconnaissance aircraft and named after Carl Vinson, a congressman and great supporter of Antarctic scientific research. Unusually, a group of climbers managed to persuade the US government to sponsor a major mountaineering expedition to Mount Vinson, and the 4,897 metre (16,065 feet) peak was climbed by a strong and well-equipped team in 1966. The mountain lies in the remote Sentinel Range of the Ellsworth Mountains, which are large enough to stand above the giant Ronne ice shelf at the base of the Antarctic Peninsula. Expeditions have continued to come here, as the mountain is one of the Seven Summits – the highest mountains on each continent – and the route has been pioneered by private mountain guides who utilize the natural blue ice runway at nearby Patriot Hills base camp.

A mountain climber approaches the peak of Mount Vinson, the highest mountain in Antarctica

Natural wonders featured in the book: